NCT Bo

Crying baby

___

Other titles in this series:

Antenatal Tests
First Foods
Potty Training
Postnatal Depression
Safe Foods
Sleep

NCT Book of

Crying baby

Anna McGrail

Thorsons
An Imprint of HarperCollins*Publishers*
in collaboration with National Childbirth Trust Publishing

Thorsons/National Childbirth Trust Publishing
Thorsons is an Imprint of HarperCollins*Publishers*
77–85 Fulham Palace Road
Hammersmith, London W6 8JB

Published by Thorsons and
National Childbirth Trust 1998

3 5 7 9 10 8 6 4 2

A catalogue record for this book
is available from the British Library

ISBN 0 7225 3609 7

Printed and bound in Great Britain by
Caledonian International Book Manufacturing Ltd, Glasgow

Contents

Introduction   vii

1   Why do babies cry?   1
2   Finding the right approach   17
3   Looking after yourself   39
4   Survival strategies   67
5   Special situations   113
6   As your baby grows . . .   133

Resources   141
Further reading   155
Index   163

About the author

Anna McGrail has edited many books and journals on health and social care issues. She is the author of the BMA-award winning *You and Your New Baby*, and *Infertility: The Last Secret*, both of which draw on her wide experience as a volunteer for the NCT. Her second novel, *Mrs Einstein*, received widespread acclaim in Europe and the USA, and she has also written radio and stage plays. Anna and her partner Pete have two children, one of whom was a 'classic' crying baby.

The National Childbirth Trust (NCT) offers support in pregnancy, childbirth and early parenthood. We aim to give every parent the chance to make informed choices.

We try to make sure that our services, activities and membership are fully accessible to everyone. Donations to our work are welcome.

Introduction

All babies cry. We've all heard babies crying before so we know what it sounds like. What can come as a shock to a new parent, however, is the way the sound of our *own* baby's crying can produce such a profound and instinctive reaction in us. When the crying goes on and on, that sound can become unbearable.

Yesterday evening, I was walking home through the park. It was a beautiful summer evening with the sun slanting low through the trees. Along the path ahead of me was a father pushing a baby in a pram. I could see a small fist waving out of the pram, then the blanket got kicked in the air, then, as I got closer, I heard the crying. A cross cry, a cry of rage. Against the trees and the sunset, how tiny it seemed. But how loud that crying must have sounded inside a house. How it must have reverberated off the walls. I would like to say that by the time we reached the park gates, the crying had subsided, but it hadn't. The baby was still cross about *something*. But the father wasn't.

The message of this book is that there *are* strategies for coping with a crying baby. We look at these in the context of normal patterns of crying, including three-month 'colic', the links with feeding and sleeping, and, more widely, the effect of a crying baby on the relationship between a couple and on family life. Parents have come forward with many ideas on how to soothe a baby, which we set out in detail, and while these may not provide you with an instant 'cure' for your baby's crying, it is possible that they might. What they are more likely to do is help you understand the reasons why babies cry, why some cry more than others and, even if you can't stop the crying, how you can cope with it. Some of the hardest things that the parents of a crying baby have to fight against are a loss of confidence in their own abilities as parents, and the frustration, depression and anger that can result. I have two children and my first, Ben, was a classic 'crying baby'. I wanted to write this book because, even though he has now grown out of it (after all, he is nine), I remember vividly the loneliness and frustration of those early days.

The parents who contributed to the book became known to me in three ways: there were parents I met in my work as a postnatal supporter with the National Childbirth Trust; there were parents who took the trouble to write to me after we put an ad in the NCT's national magazine, *New Generation*; and there were friends who contacted me when they heard I was working on the book and who wanted to say something that might just help someone else who was going through the experience.

And it is an experience that, if you haven't been through it yourself, is impossible to explain.

My thanks go to all the parents who shared their thoughts and feelings so honestly and openly and who spent time writing down the details of what life was like with their crying baby. Many of them ended their accounts with a phrase like 'I hope this helps someone'. Although their stories are often painful, the underlying message is that if you can find ways of coping with the dark days of crying, the experience may even forge a stronger bond between you and your baby. All the things in this book are meant to help, and my hope is that some of them do.

Anna McGrail
August 1998

1

Why do babies cry?

When our baby cries, few of us can ignore it. Each tiny being comes programmed with an alarm system which sets our own responses of adrenaline into motion. We rush into action because it is our deep instinct to do what we can to stop the crying. This is a natural response because crying is a survival mechanism for babies: unable to do anything for themselves, they need to provoke someone into providing them with warmth, sustenance, comfort and affection. But if we can't make the crying stop, our own heart rates and tensions increase, which can make coping with the crying even more stressful, however much we may try to deal with the situation logically.

How can we deal with it logically? We've just given birth – an exhausting experience in its own right. Besides the inevitable tiredness caused by the labour and delivery, many new mothers will be recovering from surgery, either from an episiotomy or a caesarean. Add to this one or more of the following: afterpains as the uterus contracts to its pre-delivery size, breast engorgement as the milk comes in, post-delivery bowel or urine discomfort, itchy stitches, sore nipples from a baby who won't latch on, rapidly changing hormone levels – and you have the perfect recipe for an exhausted new mother. Fathers, too, are often overwhelmed. They may be dealing with a lack of sleep and a sense of helplessness, and often have to juggle the needs of their new family with the demands of paid work sooner than they'd bargained for. And on top of this, these new parents have to cope with a baby who seems pretty unhappy to be here and who rewards their every effort to comfort or care for her with another session of yelling. No wonder logic flies out of the window.

A 'crying baby' does not exist in isolation. The crying is one strand in a tapestry of stresses, demands and adjustments to new relationships. All of these aspects needs to be considered if parents are going to first understand and then be able to cope with the rejection, frustration, anger and sorrow they often experience when their baby cries persistently.

This book will consider all these aspects but in this chapter we begin by looking at the crying itself. Crying is an essential phase in the development of every baby, and if we consider the needs that the baby is usually trying to express through the crying, then this will be the first step towards understanding.

Crying is natural

When a baby is born, her only means of communicating with us is through crying. Through crying, she has to express an enormous number of needs. In the early weeks, this crying may seem random to new parents, for no obvious reason, at no particular time, and we need to try to work out if she is hot, cold, hungry, thirsty, tired or simply in need of a cuddle.

As babies grow, however, there are other ways in which they can communicate with us, so it becomes gradually easier for us to get to know what they are saying. They get better at eye contact, making noises and cooing at you, all of which reduce the need for crying. At around the age of six weeks, babies seem to pass through a 'neurological shift'; developments in the brain and nervous system mean that they generally spend longer asleep at night, with more time awake and alert during the day. Also at around six weeks, many babies discover another effective way of communicating – smiling.

By the age of four or five months, the amount that most babies cry is significantly reduced from the early days. Even before your baby starts speaking (usually at around 12 months), she will have developed a whole range of communication and social skills, including babbling, reaching for things and laughing, which means that crying is often used as a last resort.

Getting to know your baby's needs

In the early days, however, all babies will cry. Even 'normal', 'average', entirely healthy new-borns will cry for somewhere between one and three hours each day. They have to. It is their only way of communicating their needs. These early days can be very frightening for new parents because they have not yet learned how to read their baby's cries. If we can discover *why* they are crying, then that makes life much easier because we can try to do something about it. This is not as difficult as it sounds because all babies have basic needs, and if you can ensure that these are being met, this will gradually help you to link particular kinds of cries to these particular needs.

Some of the most obvious questions to ask yourself when your baby is crying are listed in the following checklist. They all relate to a particular need of the baby. In this chapter we will review these needs and look at how they might tie in with the personality of your baby, and in the following chapters we will look at how you can find ways of meeting those needs in a way that suits you, your baby and your family.

Crying checklist

- ❑ Is she hungry?
- ❑ Is she too hot or too cold?
- ❑ Does her nappy need changing?
- ❑ Is she fed up or bored and needs entertaining?
- ❑ Does she need reassurance, or just to be held?
- ❑ Does she just want to suck something?
- ❑ Is she tired?
- ❑ Is she ill? (If there are other signs that she may be unwell, such as a rash or a high temperature, then always ask your GP to check your baby. There is more information about when to call the doctor on page 14.)

The need for food

Hunger is the most common reason for a young baby's crying and, in general, the younger a baby is, the more likely it is that she is crying because she is hungry. A small stomach cannot hold much milk at a time (at six weeks, between 75ml and 150ml will fill her up) so she needs constant replenishment. The exception to this is in the first day or two after birth when babies often feed very little. Breastfeeding mothers will be aware of this: during this time the very concentrated early milk, colostrum, is produced and the milk 'comes in' by the third day or so.

Hungry babies often cry with a distinctive rhythm which gradually becomes louder and more sustained.

Many mothers find that this crying stimulates their own hormones and triggers the let-down response if they are breastfeeding.

In addition, some babies seem to need an extra intake of milk in the late afternoon or early evening to prepare for a longer stretch of sleep. Many mothers have also noticed increased fretfulness and a need to feed more just before a 'growth spurt' (often at around six weeks, three months and between four and six months).

Therefore if your baby is crying, a sensible approach is always to offer her some milk. If she does not want it, perhaps she is expressing the next need . . .

The need to be comfortable

Like all of us, a baby will protest if her clothes are too tight, if she is too hot or too cold, or if her wet or soiled nappy is making her uncomfortable. These are all things that you can check when your baby cries.

It can help to check that your baby isn't waking from sleep simply because she's too cold (if her cot is against an outside wall, it may get chilly in the winter) or too hot (if she's next to the airing cupboard and the water heater stays on all night). Babies do not need hot rooms. A room thermometer will help to guide you in this: the ideal temperature for your baby's bedroom is around 18°C/64°F.

Using lightweight blankets in the Moses basket or crib, and in the cot, can also help you adjust the temperature by adding or removing layers as necessary.

Safe sleeping

The Foundation for the Study of Infant Death includes the following in its recommendations for reducing the risk of cot death:

- ❑ Put your baby on her back to sleep
- ❑ Put her in the 'feet to foot' position, with her feet at the foot of the cot so she can't wriggle down and cover her head with the blankets
- ❑ Don't let your baby get too hot or too cold
- ❑ Don't let anyone smoke near your baby

The need to be stimulated

If your baby isn't hungry and seems comfortable but still cries, remember that a baby can be lonely, bored and in need of a bit of entertainment, just like the rest of us. This doesn't mean that he is 'demanding' or 'attention seeking' but is as much in need of stimulation as you would be if you were tucked up for most of the day in a crib.

The need to be held

Some babies need a great deal of reassurance. Adults can be comforted by soothing words; if they can see someone in the room with them, that can be reassuring. For babies, words and sight are often not enough and they need the safety of close physical contact.

The need to suck

Many breastfeeding mothers notice that their baby enjoys 'comfort sucking' at the breast, not just sucking for purely nutritional purposes. In some babies the need to suck is very strong and you will need to find ways of meeting this need. While some babies breeze through babyhood without ever needing a dummy, finger or thumb to suck on, others will find great comfort in them. As they grow, some will also find comfort in a blanket, cuddly or special toy to chew on, and will require one or all of these items to comfort them.

The need to sleep

Babies will often cry because they need to sleep. Perhaps this is one of the needs that is most easily overlooked as we often assume that babies will just fall asleep whenever they want to. Many do – and can then sleep through anything – but others don't. If your baby is crying because she is over-stimulated and needs a rest, then all that singing, talking and jiggling about may be keeping her awake when she needs to sleep.

Birth trauma

Along with all the usual needs of babies, research shows that some babies seem to cry in order to relieve the after-effects of a difficult birth experience. If the baby has had a ventouse or forceps delivery, or if the labour was unusually slow (or unusually fast), then the stress of this may leave repercussions which the baby is trying to resolve by crying. For more information on how osteopathy may help in such situations, see Chapter 4.

Unexplained crying

If you have checked all the obvious reasons why your baby might be crying, and once the baby's particular need has been met – whether this is for milk, sleep, sucking, comfort or stimulation – the crying will often stop. Sometimes, however, it doesn't. And there just doesn't seem to be any reason why the crying carries on.

Ann's baby, Rose, was one of those who cried in no particular pattern for no obvious cause, but cried incessantly:

> 'I remember thinking that if only she came with an on/off switch, I could cope.'

Unfortunately, nature is not so obliging; as parents, we have to find other ways of reaching that 'off' switch. It is not always easy. In Chapter 4 parents share ideas about how they managed to soothe their baby when all the baby's needs seemed to have been met but the crying continued. We hope that some of these will work for you, even if you never find out the reason that your baby started crying in the first place.

What we can do here is put to rest some of the most common myths that have grown up around crying babies.

- Breastfed babies do not cry more than bottle-fed babies. Studies show that babies who are breastfed on demand do not cry any more or less than their bottle-feeding counterparts so there is rarely anything to be gained by switching from breast to bottle.
- Spooning solids into a baby will not help. Babies under three months have great difficulty in digesting anything other than milk, so solid food, far from reducing the crying, may actually make your baby more uncomfortable.
- Babies do not cry because their mothers are over-anxious or 'hostile' towards the baby. Mothers of crying babies often become anxious and hostile towards their babies, but this is a result of the crying, not a cause of it. Studies showing this go back as far as the 1960s but 'maternal anxiety' is still often cited as a reason, making an already concerned mother even more fraught.
- Babies do not cry because they are spoiled. They cry because they need something.
- First babies are no more likely to cry than subsequent babies – so you can't put it down to 'novice parenting'.
- Girls and boys cry just as much as each other.

In fact, there are very few things that predispose toward a 'crying baby'. There is some evidence that stress during pregnancy is a factor (when the mother has to deal with life-changing events like a death or illness in the family, a house move, separation from her partner, and so on) but there are women who have had dream pregnancies and come back to earth with a bump when their baby cries, and there are also women who have moved house, changed jobs and dealt with extreme family crises all in the same pregnancy who find their babies placid and a pleasure to have around.

One very important element seems to be the baby's own temperament. As all parents realise from the moment their first child is born, every baby has their own distinct personality from the start.

Getting to know your baby's character

We are all born different. Some babies will be sunny natured almost immediately after birth, others will be placid and sleepy. Some babies, unfortunately, seem very unhappy or cross, and 'miserable' is a term that their parents use quite freely. I spoke to quite a few parents of 'miserable' babies who felt that their babies were unhappy simply because they were a baby; as they grew older and gained more independence, learning to crawl, sit, stand and walk, some of the frustrations of babyhood disappeared, although there were many tearful months before this was achieved.

Hayley's baby, Sylvie, was prone to crying but in a very 'sad' way:

'My mother used to call Sylvie "Queen Victoria" because nothing ever made her smile. Not for want of trying on our part. She just wasn't ready to smile for several months.'

Temperament does seem to affect the amount that a baby cries and some really do cry more than others. Maria, after some thought, decided that the only word to sum up her baby's character was 'angry':

'I was running around like someone demented, offering George milk, water, juice, toys, music, mobiles, and nothing seemed right. He was cross, cross with me, the world, with everything. It wasn't until he started sitting, then crawling, then walking that the anger began to subside. By then I'd recognised the pattern and was more able to deal with it.'

Also, it seems to take some babies a long time simply to get used to the world. After the calm warm waters of the womb, they need to adjust to a world full of brightness, sights, sounds, colours and unfamiliar sensations, as Colleen found out:

'Rory goes into the startle reflex over the smallest things. He's just a nervous baby, as if everything is a surprise to him.'

Nervous babies often cry more than average for some months before they develop any confidence in the world, and have a great need for comfort and reassurance. It is only as you gradually get to know your baby that you can adapt to her particular character and be more confident about interpreting her needs.

Some babies who seem especially 'difficult' are often described as 'high-need' babies. They are intense, demanding, need lots of physical contact, want to comfort-suck frequently and generally demand a high level of attention from their parents. If your baby is like this, remember that they are needs that she is expressing and these needs won't go away if you ignore them. The intense parenting that these babies require can be exhausting and the more resources, support and help you can call on, the better.

Fears about 'spoiling' the baby

When a baby cries, her heart rate increases, oxygen levels in the blood decrease, and she becomes steadily more distressed. It takes much longer to calm a tiny baby who has been crying for ten minutes than to calm a baby who has been crying for two. In the early days, most parents instinctively feel it is right to respond to crying quickly, although many worry that they are 'spoiling' their babies in the process.

As babies grow, and come to a greater understanding of the world around them, their crying does change. Who has not seen a two-year-old wail pitifully for another bar of chocolate? But small babies can't be manipulative like that. For them, the links between cause and effect are hazy at best. They cannot think to themselves, 'If I just cry a bit louder then she'll have to come'. They are not crying because they are 'demanding' or 'fussy'. They are simply crying because they need something and this is the only way they can let you know it.

You cannot spoil your baby by trying to meet her

needs. In fact, some research has shown that babies whose needs are not met when they are tiny become more demanding as they grow, not less. So if you instinctively pick your baby up whenever she cries, and comfort her, you can do so without worrying that you're 'storing up problems' for yourself in the future. In fact, you'll be avoiding them.

Should I call the doctor?

First-time parents often find it particularly hard to tell whether their baby is crying relentlessly because he is just miserable, or whether there is something more serious wrong. All babies cry; and don't forget, for some, straight-forward yelling for up to two or three hours in any one day (although it may seem like longer) is perfectly normal.

It's often only experience that will tell you how to recognise the different tone of an ill baby's cry. Conversely, when a usually noisy baby goes suddenly quiet it may be the first sign of something wrong. Any difficulty in breathing is always serious, so call your doctor immediately if you notice this in your baby.

Also, always call your doctor if diarrhoea, vomiting or constipation accompany the crying.

Call your doctor at once if:

❑ your baby is listless or floppy and uncharacteristically quiet, crying much less than normal
❑ your baby suddenly cries in an urgent tone that you have never heard before
❑ your baby's cry becomes unusually high-pitched
❑ your baby's crying becomes particularly fretful or insistent
❑ your baby seems to have difficulty breathing between his cries.

The most important thing to remember is that nobody knows your baby as well as you do. If you think there is something wrong, take her along to the surgery or give the doctor a call. Every good doctor will take your concerns seriously.

Health professionals see a lot of crying babies and in most cases there is nothing physically wrong with them. There are cases, however, where a baby's crying has been discovered to be caused by an undiagnosed urinary tract infection or unstable hip joints, for example. If you feel that there may be a physical problem underlying your baby's continuing crying, it is worth asking for a second opinion, as Michele found:

'I took Georgia to a casualty department after seeing midwives, health visitors and my GP, who all told me she had severe colic. At last, at three months, she was diagnosed as having a digestive reflux problem and was given medication which eased the situation substantially.'

It is also worth checking with your doctor if the crying was of late onset (it began after one month of age) or is continuing past the 'colic barrier' of three months. GPs can help to rule out any physical or developmental problems and put your mind at rest that there is no underlying reason you have overlooked.

In addition, GPs and health visitors are always willing to talk to parents whose baby cries excessively. If you are becoming exhausted from the crying, or you are suffering from a prolonged lack of sleep, it is worth talking to your GP about strategies that can help your family. Both GPs and health visitors can put you in touch with further sources of advice and support.

2

Finding the right approach

Many babies seem to have a few calm days after the birth, only letting you know whether they are going to be a 'crying baby' round about day three. Others have difficulty settling from the start, as Nicole remembers:

> 'Those first weeks with Emily were hell. From the moment she was born, she cried. In hospital, they called her "the pest" and when she got home, it was no better.'

A difficulty in 'settling' seems to be especially common if the labour has been prolonged or interventions were needed. David was Jane's second baby:

> 'He was over a week late and I was induced with pessaries. The labour was far more painful than the first time, and I needed a forceps delivery. Unfortunately

the cord was round his neck and, as I'd had pethidine 40 minutes before his arrival, we were not off to a good start. David was restless from the beginning, not settling at all for 15 hours after birth.'

Yet there is no clear correlation between birth experience and later crying, as Jane herself realised. Esther is her fifth baby:

'Esther was full term and four days, a normal delivery with gas and air for pain relief. I was hopeful that we had "cracked" the colic problem. But Esther cried solidly for six months.'

Some mothers find that they cope well while they're in hospital, but going home is a different matter:

'I had postnatal complications which resulted in ten days in hospital. In hospital, Natalie slept lots and breastfed four-hourly almost to the minute. Once I got home, things seemed to go to pieces. I struggled both physically and emotionally. When she cried, I just held her, unable to know what to do.'   *Cathy*

Most anxieties in the early days revolve around feeding the baby, holding the baby and sleep. If you can find the right approach that works for you in these areas, you will be much better equipped to cope with the demands of looking after a new-born, whether she cries or not.

Feeding

Breastfeeding is the ideal way to feed your baby, not only in terms of its nutritional value, but also because of the antibodies in breast milk, its instant availability without the need for complicated equipment and the fact that it's free. Yet for many mothers of crying babies, breastfeeding seems to be at the heart of their problems.

Establishing breastfeeding is an art; some of us have a knack, whereas others find that we need support, encouragement and hints on technique before we have mastered it. The first few days can be difficult, especially if we feel self-conscious about it and reluctant to try our new skills in the presence of visitors.

Even today mothers get worried that they should be feeding by the clock and worry when their baby cries more frequently than, say, every four hours. This can be reinforced by comments from friends and relatives along the lines of, 'He's not crying *again* is he?' If this happens to you, you may like to recall that the idea of 'schedule' feeding was generated by the prevalent use of bottle-feeding in the not-too-distant past. Mothers and babies stayed in hospital for up to a week with nurses responsible for much of the infant feeding. The babies were put on a schedule simply to ensure that each one got fed.

These days babies stay with their parents most of the time, so the logic behind schedule feeding disappears, not least because babies don't know how to tell the time. They only know whether they're hungry or not.

New-born babies do need to be fed frequently. A baby

who needs to be fed every two to three hours (measured from the beginning of one feed to the beginning of the next) will mean that you could be giving eight to twelve feeds a day. Many women worry that frequent feeding means that their babies aren't getting enough milk – especially as with breastfeeding you can't see how much is going in – and become even more convinced of this when the baby doesn't seem to settle easily after a feed.

One of the most common patterns I found when talking to new mothers ran along the lines of Jane's experience:

> 'Over the few days after David's birth, a pattern developed: he would breastfeed for 10–15 minutes, fall asleep for 5–10 minutes, wake and be quiet for 3–4 minutes, then scream continually until the next breastfeed, sleep, wake and scream again. This continued for 16 weeks.'

Many other mothers spoke of their babies spending long periods at the breast – one or two hours was not unusual – and yet still not being able to settle. With such prolonged feeding, too, it is more likely that nipples will become sore and the experience will become less and less pleasant.

To understand what might lie behind this pattern, we need to look closely at what happens when we are breastfeeding. When the baby starts to suckle, he will begin by getting the milk that is stored in the ducts just behind the nipple. This is called the 'foremilk'. It is thirst-quenching and rich in protein. As the sucking continues, it stimulates the release of oxytocin into your bloodstream, which causes the muscles further back in your breast to contract and 'let down' the hindmilk. Some women feel this let-down reflex very strongly when they are feeding. The hindmilk is richer in fat and contains more calories and will satisfy the baby better. It is the let-down reflex that causes the production of more milk, enough to meet your baby's growing needs.

Key to successful breastfeeding in the early days, there-fore, is to make sure that the baby stimulates the let-down reflex and receives enough of the rich hindmilk to make his stomach feel full. This enables him to settle into a deep sleep until he is ready for his next feed and/or a bit of social interaction.

In some cases, the baby may not be receiving enough of the rich hindmilk to make him feel full even though he is suckling for hours. Instead, he is receiving only the sugar-rich foremilk which passes very quickly through his digestive system, causing wind and stomach cramps on the way. A few minutes later, he starts to cry . . . and is offered the breast again. How can you ensure that your baby does get the hindmilk that he needs? There are strategies, key to which is recognising that when your very young baby cries, he may need comfort rather than food. If you offer him a finger to suck, for example, you may be able to keep him calm for a couple of hours until he does feel hungry and he will then have room in his stomach for a long feed which includes the essential hind-milk. This worked for Kya whose baby, Kiri, at five days of age, had developed this distressing pattern:

'I'd asked the breastfeeding counsellor to come to help me get Kiri latched on as I was getting very sore and wanted to make sure I was getting the position right. Kiri was thrashing about and crying and I was sure she must be starving. Instead, the breastfeeding counsellor suggested I find other ways of calming her, and Kiri sucked on my little finger for a while, eventually falling off to sleep. When she did wake, a couple of hours later, she fed much better than she ever had before and I began to feel confident that I could satisfy her.'

Malathi, whose baby Gayatri had developed 'colic' at around six days old, felt that all her time was spent feeding Gayatri or rocking her off to sleep, and she was at her wits' end:

'My health visitor, when she saw us, suggested that I try to space feeds out more as Gayatri seemed to be feeding almost constantly. So I walked her up and down, patted her back, didn't constantly offer her a feed, and her feeding gradually settled down into much longer intervals, with much less crying as well.'

If you are breastfeeding, don't automatically decide that you aren't making enough milk for your baby if he is crying and immediately stop. Try spacing feeds out more by offering comfort for a while so that the baby takes 'a good feed' next time. If you feel that your baby does need extra milk, talk to a breastfeeding counsellor about ways to increase your milk supply.

How do you tell if your baby is getting enough to eat?

A content and happy baby is an obvious giveaway, and you may not feel the need to get her weighed to check that she is growing well. A regular supply of wet nappies is another reliable sign, although breast milk is so well absorbed that there may be no regular bowel movements, just a yellow stain on the nappy.

Weight gain is another indicator, although most babies lose weight in the first few days, some up to 10% of their birth weight. This is usually regained by two weeks of age. Sometimes, however, the pattern of weight gain can cause more alarm than reassurance. Babies can gain weight erratically: a lot some weeks, none the next. It is only regular weighing that can signal whether your baby is gaining weight steadily or not, and whether hunger may be a cause of distress. Sue found this when she noticed an increase in Simon's crying at around eight weeks of age:

'As Simon is a very large baby, the health visitor questioned whether I was managing to keep up with feeding him. His weight graph showed a dip, which did suggest that he might be getting miserable because he was hungry. I was faced with the choice of sitting around, resting, in order to make enough milk or supplementing his breastfeeds with some bottles. I decided on the latter. Lo and behold Simon's weight picked up and he went back to being the happy soul he'd been before.'

For some mothers, the decision to bottle-feed is not so easy, especially if they have been determined to breastfeed, as Sharon reports:

'Breastfeeding just developed into a miserable experience. My partner was supportive, holding Kieron while I tried to get him latched on, and the midwives gave me every encouragement, but my nipples became so sore that each feed was painful. Both Kieron and I ended up crying every time and I began to dread it when he was hungry. At the same time, I felt guilty about not enjoying breastfeeding and was overwhelmed by my feelings of failure. I struggled on for two weeks before giving him formula but once I did my relationship with him, and with my partner, suddenly changed. Life wasn't a daily anxious trial any more, and that was very important to us as a family.'

There are several organisations, as well as your midwife and health visitor, which can offer you encouragement and support if you're finding breastfeeding difficult, and these are listed on page 142. The NCT, for example, has trained breastfeeding counsellors who can give you information on every aspect, from correct positioning to expressing to weaning. This support is freely available whether you are an NCT member or not.

If you are bottle-feeding your baby, then provided the formula is made up in the correct proportions and in the right amounts for your baby's age and weight, she will probably not be crying because she is hungry. Check with your health visitor if you are worried, and read the instructions carefully on how to make up the formula. If she is going through a growth spurt, she may want to be offered a bottle more often and you may find that smaller bottles, offered more frequently, will help. Changing your brand of formula may help, and your health visitor will be able to give you plenty of advice on this. Be wary, however, of changing to a formula advertised as being for 'hungrier' babies. There are two standard types of formula milk – whey dominant, sometimes known as first-stage milk, and casein dominant, known as second-stage or 'follow-on' milk. First-stage milk has a casein:whey ratio of 40:60, the same as breast milk. With second-stage milk, the casein:whey ratio is 80:20. It is aimed at babies from six months and is promoted as being more satisfying because it takes longer to digest. However, first-stage milk is perfectly suitable for babies up until about a year old, and switching milks too early can cause constipation.

> If you are bottle-feeding your baby, do not be tempted to add an extra scoop to a bottle to 'help him settle'. It will overload his system with salts and could be dangerous.

While breastfed babies do not need any extra fluids, a bottle-fed baby may become thirsty and may need extra boiled and cooled water, especially in the hot summer months, or if he has become overheated at night.

Wind

Along with feeding comes wind. Wind is caused when a baby swallows some air while feeding. Wind is only a problem if it causes your baby stomach pains, and unfortunately it does seem to cause many babies a lot of discomfort.

Cathy's first baby was badly affected:

'Natalie would breastfeed for long periods . . . three-quarters of an hour was not unusual. With Natalie I didn't worry so much about wind because the books say breastfed babies rarely get wind. I believed them. But, looking back, I think she was suffering from wind. I think this because of my second baby, Colin; the one immediate difference between them is that he burps! He breastfeeds for ten minutes, I hold him up, rub his back, he burps and settles.'

Some babies are highly resistant to anything that could be interpreted as 'winding'. This is what Dara found:

'Wind dominated our lives those first few weeks and made us all miserable. I spent all my time patting his back, rubbing his shoulders, moving him about, trying to get the wind out so he could settle and sleep, but with no success. And when Ben did drop off, I knew he'd only be asleep for five minutes before he started getting uncomfortable, squirming around and yelling. So I'd start the whole process once more and walk him round and round until he needed feeding again.'

To keep wind to a minimum, you may like to try the following:

- ❏ Feed your baby in a more upright position
- ❏ If you are breastfeeding, make sure she is latched on properly before she begins to suck
- ❏ If you are bottle-feeding, try a different shape or size of teat
- ❏ Shifting positions mid-feed – the movement may cause your baby to burp and she then has more room in her stomach for more milk
- ❏ Keep her upright after a feed, perhaps over your shoulder, to encourage her to burp out the air

---

Gripe waters and other preparations seem to have little real effect, although many parents try them as they like to feel they are doing something to help their baby. If your baby seems to suffer from wind, soothing him so that he doesn't swallow yet more air when crying may be the most effective solution. It is something that babies 'grow out of', almost without you noticing, although this can seem like a long time.

Clingy babies

Many babies seem to crave constant human contact to the extent that their parents call them 'Velcro babies'. Kate could see that this was the case with Alice:

> 'She cried unless she was in physical contact with either her dad or me and in the first few weeks it had to be me. She was always very aware of my presence, or lack of it, so we carried her around wherever we went in the house.'

> 'From a very young age Natalie was "mummy-clingy" and wanted to be held, especially by me. Try and put her in a pushchair, car seat or cot and I could rely on a crying session.'
> *Cathy*

Cathy and her partner developed ways of living with Natalie's demands:

> 'We bed-shared, I used a baby sling then a back-carrier rather than a pram. For long journeys, we travelled by train.'

Yet Natalie's need to be held took its toll:

> 'I know some philosophies believe this close contact between new-borns and mothers is natural, even essential, and for me it was certainly the only way to stop her crying. But I felt totally absorbed,

restricted and trapped by the situation. It was not a happy first year.'

If you can accept that wanting to be close to you all the time is a need that your baby has, and not an unreasonable request, then you may be able to cope with it better. Cope with the demands it makes on you by sharing the load with others as much as you can, and making sure that you do get some time to yourself to meet your own needs, too.

Sleeping

New-borns tend to sleep somewhere between 14 and 20 hours out of the 24, usually in short stretches, and without any regard for whether it's morning or the middle of the night. Learning the difference between day and night is something most babies need to be taught, and there are ways in which you can help them with this, but don't expect it to happen instantly. Also in the early days, babies won't be able to sleep through the night without a feed. For these reasons, therefore, broken nights are an inevitable phase of parenthood, although for some parents the phase lasts longer than others. While some lucky parents find that their child sleeps through the night from the age of three months or so, others will find that broken nights persist much longer.

Helping to distinguish between night and day

❏ Darken the room so it's obviously different from daytime.
❏ Make night feeds as calm and unstimulating as possible.
❏ Encourage play and interaction during the day, not at night.

If you have made sure that all your baby's other needs are met, and nothing soothes your baby after about half an hour of fruitless attempts, your baby may be trying to go to sleep. What can you do?

Kate realised what she had to do very early on:

'Within a few days of Alice's arrival we realised that the only way we were going to cope with night-times was by having her in bed with us. She cuddled up to one or the other of us and helped herself to frequent feeds from me.'

You can keep outside stimulation to a minimum while she finds her own way into sleep. Wrap her up securely and either simply sit and hold her or put her on her back in her basket or crib and wait. It won't happen instantly, and this is where you need to make a decision. Either you stay with her, but recognise that sleep will eventually come, or, if you find listening to the crying unbearable, go into a different room, close the door and focus on something else.

If the crying is still going on 15 minutes later, however, pick her up again and try soothing activities based on meeting her other needs. Offer her milk, change her nappy . . .

Many parents find the idea of leaving their baby to cry herself to sleep appalling. Others decide that the respite from the crying is worth it, because then they can save their strength and patience for when their baby needs them for other things.

However you decide to help your baby to get to sleep, recognising that her need for sleep may be the only reason she is crying may help you through some difficult days.

Remember:

- ❑ If you are leaving your baby to go to sleep on her own, make sure that you have placed her on her back.
- ❑ Don't place your baby face-down.
- ❑ Do not use a sheepskin for your baby to sleep on because of the risk of overheating.

Help your baby settle

Although babies need to be held when they are crying, they don't need to be held all the time. If you rock your baby every time she goes to sleep, she won't learn how to go to sleep without your rocking her. To avoid this happening, try putting your baby in her cot when she is drowsy but not crying, and let her learn to fall asleep on her own. In this way, you may prevent secondary sleep problems later on.

Helping your baby settle alone

❏ Put your baby in her cot while she is sleepy but still awake, so that she learns that she can fall asleep on her own safely and securely.

❏ Lie your baby on her back. Older babies will find their own sleeping position but as the risk of cot death in babies over six months is extremely low this is not a worry.

❏ Place her with her feet at the end of the cot so that she can't wake herself up suddenly by pushing herself against the headboard or by wriggling too far down under the blankets (which could also make her dangerously hot).

After about six months, your baby will probably not need to feed so often at night. It can be a real boost to you all as a family if you can help her drop the night-time feeds. Unfortunately, this is not always as easy as it sounds. As Karin explains, she found herself taking a step backwards:

'First of all, Megan always went to sleep at the breast in the evening, and then again in the middle of the night. Then, as she got older, we decided to replace this night-time breastfeed with a bottle-feed because Martin could give her this and that meant my sleep wouldn't have to be broken every night. We also hoped it would help her sleep longer into the morning. But eventually she could only drop off while bottle-feeding, so that didn't seem to be getting us anywhere. So we replaced the bottle with a dummy, but that kept falling out when she was asleep and, when she woke, she'd cry until one of us got up to find it . . . so eventually she was waking every hour throughout the night and driving us crazy in the process.'

The solution that Karin found worked for her was a method often called the 'controlled crying' approach, or 'sleep training'.

The 'controlled crying' approach

Controlled crying is a way of teaching your baby to go to sleep on her own so that, if she does wake in the night, she will be able to go back to sleep without your help. Once your baby is a few months old, she doesn't need to wake in the night for a feed, so, if she is doing this, it is out of habit rather than need, and the aim is to break that habit. Controlled crying aims to reassure both you and the baby that she is all right, but that night-time is for sleeping.

❑ Settle your baby in her cot, sleepy but awake, and leave the room.
❑ If she cries, wait five minutes before returning.
❑ When you return, do not pick her up but reassure her (rub her back, stroke her head, give her a kiss, or talk to her gently), then leave again.
❑ If she continues to cry, wait ten minutes this time before returning and reassure her as before.
❑ Gradually increase the time between visits by five minutes each time, until your baby falls asleep.
❑ Expect to repeat this routine for a few nights (perhaps only one or two, but it could take a week or more) until your baby learns that she can fall asleep on her own.

It works more quickly if you carry out the controlled crying approach during daytime naps as well.

This was an approach first suggested to Mary by her GP:

'He said, "Have you ever tried leaving her for five minutes?" I was shocked and horrified. You can't leave a baby crying! "Just go into another room away from the noise for five minutes and pick her up then." I did manage to wait – one minute. The next time two, before picking Daisy up. The difference was amazing. Often she would go back to sleep before I got there, but when she was genuinely hungry I found she didn't.'

Controlled crying is an approach that also worked for Debra with Scott, her second child:

'Scott woke several times a night for breastfeeds until he was nine months old, when I just couldn't stand the tiredness any more. He cried for about an hour altogether the first time he woke, and I stayed just outside the door in case his cry changed to one of difficulty rather than anger. This happened a second time that night. The second night he slept through, and has continued to do so.'

Interestingly, Rachel, Debra's fourth child, also cried a great deal at night, but with Rachel the approach was less successful:

'I went in and out of the room at ten-minute intervals to reassure her of my presence, but I never managed to make her sleep through and the crying disturbed the rest of the family. Eventually she started coming into our bed more (she had fed and slept with me in the early days), where she was never a problem and when she was there, slept through.'

Controlled crying is a method that many parents find difficult to contemplate, and some find their baby's crying so intense that they are unable to carry it through. Yet Karin took the long-term view:

'It was awful listening to Megan cry. Just awful. But, after three nights we could see that it was working. And I knew that it would be better for her to get a good night's sleep in the long run, rather than waking up continually. And it was better for Martin and me because we were happier as parents, so that had to be good for Megan, too.'

If you are thinking of using the controlled crying method, you may like to talk to your health visitor first, for reassurance beforehand and support during the time you are carrying out your resolutions. Some babies may wake three or four times in a night and take more than an hour to settle each time, so it is easy to become discouraged and uncertain. If you can share the load with your partner, this can help you get some sleep and the emotional support you will need.

Transitions

Many parents keep their baby in their bed or in a cot in their room until she seems ready to leave (which may not be until she is three, four . . . or even older).

However, most parents decide that this is not for them. Perhaps there is another baby on the way and you want to help your child adjust in good time. Perhaps you feel that disturbed nights needn't be quite so frequent any more; for example, if she has slept in your bed since birth but now, at four or five months, she is keeping you both awake with her kicking, you may want to move her to a cot. Or she may have been sleeping in a cot in your room but now she is waking less at night, so you would like to move her to a room of her own so that you can have some space together again as a couple.

There are various combinations, but many babies between the ages of three and six months need to make a transition in their night-time arrangements, and this can trigger off a phase of renewed crying, grizzling and night-time waking.

Remember that your baby will be unsettled by the transition, so you need to give her time to adjust, but remember also that you need to teach her, gently but firmly, that this new sleeping arrangement is here to stay.

Changeover strategies

❑ Try putting her Moses basket or carry-cot inside the cot for a few nights, so that she becomes used to her new surroundings while still comforted by the safety of the familiar.

❑ If you are moving your baby to a room of her own, make sure you spend some time with her in there before leaving her alone to sleep there. For example, change her nappies in there, or show her some new mobiles above the cot.

❑ Give any night feeds in the baby's room, or sitting up in a chair in your room so that she doesn't come to associate feeding with drifting back off to sleep in your bed.

❑ Ease the transition by putting something of yours in the cot, such as a T-shirt you've worn, as she may find the smell comforting.

Yet no matter how well you've prepared for the transition, it is likely that it will spark off some crying, and you may find that the 'controlled crying' method gives you the confidence to see through the transition.

3

Looking after yourself

The 'baby blues'

Many new mothers go through a low phase in the first two or three days after the birth of their baby, often called the 'baby blues' – it's an almost universal experience. At this stage anything can set you off weeping, even if it's just the arrival of a congratulations card. Baby blues may be linked to hormonal changes as your body abruptly stops producing the high levels of hormones needed to nourish the baby through the placenta and starts to produce the hormones needed for breastfeeding instead. No one can expect to adjust to all these physical changes without some emotional changes as well, but a feeling of tearfulness and depression is also undoubtedly also linked to the pressures of looking after a young baby:

'Those first few days were awful. Holly wouldn't latch on, my scar was leaking, my breasts were sore, Holly couldn't settle and just kept up this plaintive moan all the time. It was worse because I'd expected to feel so happy and all I could feel was miserable.'

Clare

Anxiety and stress are not just confined to mothers, however. Andy, who became a father relatively late in life, remembers how shocked he was by his daughter Isobel's crying:

'I was going to be the perfect parent, was going to make sure that Isobel was always happy. When she cried, she seemed so angry, as if she was accusing me of not loving her enough. It shattered all my expectations.'

The baby blues are not the same as postnatal depression, which is a more severe illness, affecting approximately one in ten women. Baby blues are transitory and soon disappear. 'Postnatal depression' describes a collection of symptoms which occur a few weeks after the birth; they range from exhaustion and irritability through persistent depression. At the extreme end of the spectrum is an illness called puerperal psychosis, where the lives of mother and baby may be at risk, although this affects only approximately two new mothers in every thousand. Many mothers of crying babies, however, experience symptoms in the middle range, when the feelings of constant exhaustion contribute to a depression that will not lift. At first, it can be hard to realise that this is depression and not just tired-ness, and often partners or relatives will not know how the mother really feels:

> 'I didn't tell anyone how awful things were. I was tired, couldn't eat, seemed to be breastfeeding con-stantly, even when he did fall asleep I couldn't though I was dropping with exhaustion, couldn't manage to do even the simplest things right, but I put everything down to his crying. I thought that if I could just find the key to stop that, then every-thing would be all right again. I used to make a special effort when the midwife or health visitor came round because I didn't want to admit to any-one that I just wasn't coping.'   *Tanya*

Liz experienced something similar:

> 'I kept telling myself, "Pull yourself together. Pull yourself together." I kept saying, "You are a lucky person to have this baby." But it didn't make the slightest bit of difference.'

'Tired all the time . . . '

One of the most common pieces of advice given to a new mother who is tired all the time is to 'sleep when the baby sleeps'. I have never met a mother who managed this more than once (I only managed it once myself, and that was when the effects of the general anaesthetic were still in my system). I have certainly never met a mother of a crying baby who managed it on a regular basis.

> 'Both my GP and health visitor came out with this pearl of wisdom, and this was after I had already pointed out that Scott never settled for more than ten or 15 minutes at a time.'   *Eleanor*

Dara found it difficult to give herself permission to slow down:

> 'The thing is, when you have a new baby in the house, there are lots of extra jobs to get done, not fewer. In the short spells when Ben wasn't crying, there were things I had to do, like buy bread and milk, clean my teeth . . . There was no way I could slip between the sheets, however much I felt like I wanted to.'

If your baby sleeps little and cries a lot, it doesn't take long for exhaustion to set in, as Siobhan recalls:

> 'Our first six months with Maeve were dreadful. Day after day I would wake up crying, knowing that this was the best I was going to feel all day. I felt like someone had attached lead weights to my hands and feet. I dragged myself through the house. If Maeve did seem to settle for a moment, I could hardly bear to close my eyes because I knew that the crying would begin again the instant I began to drift off.'

'Every day was one of frustration for me. I felt I couldn't get anything done, that Rochelle wouldn't stop crying or fall asleep ever, that I was a mess and couldn't go anywhere or do anything about it. I was often very tearful.'   *Veronica*

Eleanor eventually found a way to cope with her feelings of failure:

'I realised that some days just getting a load of laundry done was a major achievement. I wasn't getting done half the things I wanted to do because nearly all my day was taken up with walking up and down trying to comfort Scott. Each day I made a list of things I really wanted to get done – laundry, dishes, shopping – and prioritised them. Then I crossed off whatever was at the bottom of the list. It just wasn't important enough to worry about.'

Keep healthy

A baby's constant crying can wear anyone down, but if you're making sure that you're taking care of yourself, too, you will have more energy and resilience to cope with the added strains and stresses that a crying baby can impose.

Ensure that you continue to eat a varied diet. It is easy to forget to look after ourselves in the postnatal period, after being so careful in pregnancy. In particular, iron-rich foods can help you combat the risk of anaemia and restore your energy levels so that you're more able to cope with the crying. The box below shows some iron-rich snacks that will help you through the day.

Sensible snacks

- ❑ A bowl of cereal
- ❑ A jacket potato topped with baked beans
- ❑ Scrambled egg on toast
- ❑ A sardine sandwich
- ❑ A handful of dried apricots, dates or sultanas with a glass of orange juice.

When Paula found that she was tired and light-headed all the time, her GP took a blood test:

'When he phoned through with the result, he thought I'd be in bed because I was so anaemic he was recommending a blood transfusion. Instead, I was putting Kirsten in her pram to go and get some shopping done at last. I'd been tired for so long and put it down to the broken nights. I took iron pills instead and although my system took a while to adjust to them, I soon felt much more able to cope.'

If you can maintain a steady blood-sugar level, you will find that this also helps to combat the feelings of tiredness. This simply means eating little and often. In our worry about the baby's feeding, it's easy to forget that we have to eat, too. Rather than add to your stress by not eating all day and then peeling potatoes and chopping vegetables to produce a traditional dinner on the dot of 6pm every evening, try having an apple here, a sandwich there, a baked potato and cheese for lunch . . . and if anyone wants anything else they can provide it themselves.

Sharing the load

Looking after a crying baby is stressful and that stress can further upset the baby . . . who cries more. Majella could tell from the start that her own stress had an adverse effect on Marisa:

> 'Possibly the worst thing was allowing her to sense how stressed I was. It made her instantly worse. But the stress of always trying to convey a sense of calmness and love was its own nightmare.'

This vicious circle is not always easy to break, and it is something that Veronica, who is a single parent, could only recognise in retrospect:

> 'I feel now that much of Rochelle's crying was in response to my own fear and anxiety about the responsibility of looking after this baby. Having seen many other crying babies, I am sure that incessant crying is often linked to an unhappy or fearful mother.'

As we stressed before, however, it is usually the baby's crying that leads to an unhappy mother, not the other way round, although once the crying begins, cause and effect seem indistinguishable and can have severe emotional consequences. Debra recognised the two things that were making her bad experience worse:

'When I didn't see enough other people to detract from the emotional intensity and when our home routine became too rigid, with me trying to get meals to the table on time, for example.'

If the crying is wearing you down, this is not the time to set the highest standards for household management, or to demand that you reach unachievable goals in any aspect of your life. Veronica can see this now:

'I was trying to live up to expectations of myself which were far too high. I was never good enough or doing well enough. I dropped old acquaintances, feeling ashamed of what I had become compared to when they knew me. I wanted to be the best mother, and took a Montessori training course so that I could teach Rochelle the "right" way.'

Sharing the load can be a life-saver, as Ali found:

'I only coped because my partner and I would take turns. Matt would rock Hannah to sleep at night when I had finished feeding her, so I could get some sleep before she woke again.'

Yet, for Ali and Matt, further support was necessary:

> 'After a week of no sleep, we were suicidal. I was in a major depression. A friend came in and rocked Hannah for five hours one night so that we could sleep. Then Matt's parents came to stay for a week and spent a long time rocking her.'

As Michele points out, it's not always easy to accept help when it is offered:

> 'It's easy to convince yourself that you have a very difficult child that only you can cope with. Give yourself a break. If anyone offers to take your baby for a short while, let them do it. Even if your child does scream all the way round the park, your neighbour or friend will be hearing it with fresh ears and won't mind half as much as you do.'

If you have a crying baby, now is also the time to make the most of your family. It is easier if they live close by and can take the baby for an hour or two, but even if they live further away, they can help. While you may feel that inflicting your crying baby on a relative, however sympathetic, is the last thing you ought to do, many parents find that a few days away works wonders. This is something that finally worked for Ali:

> 'I went to stay with my mother (because she couldn't come to our house). While I was there all I had to do was feed Hannah, and this was the start of learning

to cope. I went home for a month, and then back to my mother's to stay for another week. While we were there, my mother taught me how to get Hannah to sleep in the pram in the daytime. This was the key to my sanity.'

If you can get a different perspective on your baby's crying, it may be the breakthrough you need. Michele takes this a step further:

'Don't try to protect other people from your crying baby. If it annoys your partner or your neighbours that your baby is yelling in the night, hard luck. A crying baby can be a 24-hour nightmare for a mother, but they have other things in their lives they can take refuge in and, besides, chemists sell very good ear plugs. You can apologise, explain you are doing all you can and ask for some support.'

Naomi, too, feels that recognition of the situation by other people helped her:

'Acknowledgement by other people that it was happening and that it was awful made me feel much less alone.'

As Carla found, other people can find it difficult to accept what you're telling them. Her baby, Hassan, was prone to very violent fits and rages until he was two years old:

'Nine times out of ten I was on my own when it

happened. Even my partner had trouble believing me. He couldn't understand why Hassan and I were both so exhausted.'

Vicky and Oliver decided that, second time round, they were going to share the sleepless nights equally:

'With Sam, we quarrelled and agonised together over the unending broken crying nights. Now, if Jack cries at night, Oliver goes and sleeps in the spare room if it's his night off, or I do if it's mine. It's fair, it's convenient, and it means we're not both shattered through lack of sleep.'

Majella, too, feels that she only coped because of the support of her partner, Mike:

'Mike held Marisa every evening and weekends, as well as when she woke in the night. Holding her semi-upright on his chest seemed to soothe her. I held her the rest of the time.'

Ryan describes how he tried to offer support to his partner, Joyanne, when their son Liam had colic:

'I'd take Liam and walk him up and down, but when it came to feeding, there was little I could do to help. Sometimes I might say to Joyanne, "Shall I see if he'll take his dummy now?" if he started howling while breastfeeding, or "Do you want me to take him downstairs for a while?" I felt utterly useless, but Joyanne said later that having me there and trying to help gave her a lot of support and encouragement to go on with breastfeeding at a difficult time.'

Couples can also give each other some 'time off'. This does not mean time to catch up on the laundry but time to do something for yourself. If you can manage to spend some time away from the baby, even if it is only an hour a week, you will feel refreshed and reinvigorated by the change:

'I used to go to a yoga class once a week, which really calmed me down, and I felt the relaxation benefits lasted across the week.'   *Helen*

Sometimes we can't even manage an hour but, as Majella says, even ten minutes 'out of earshot' gave her a break. If you put aside ten minutes a day to do some exercise (and ten minutes each day is much better than an hour once a week when it comes to exercise), then you will not only feel fitter and more energetic, but, as Jan did, possibly more cheerful, too:

'As the toning effects became apparent on my post-natal stomach, I felt much less out of control all round. It was an area of my life where I could actually see improvement. I wouldn't wait for the crying to stop, I'd put Judith in her car seat and put the video on really loud, and she could watch me. Sometimes she was intrigued enough to stop grizzling for a while.'

Many swimming pools and health clubs have crèche facilities where you can leave a baby long enough to have a quick dip or workout, and you may feel that this is a worthwhile investment:

> 'A swim always did me good, though sometimes Ben couldn't let up in his crying for long enough for me to get as much exercise as I liked. I'd be swimming along in mid-length when this voice would come over the tannoy: "Will the mother of Ben please come to the crèche . . . " '   *Dara*

What you must do, however, as Sushma points out, is avoid setting yourself up to fail at something all over again:

> 'I tried to diet and couldn't keep it going, joined fitness classes, and couldn't keep it up, so felt a failure whichever way I turned. If only I could have taken the opposite view, been pleased with myself for having done a bit of exercise, rather than angry with myself for not doing more, then I might even have found the energy to keep going.'

Amy also feels this strongly:

> 'I think, when you have to cope with a crying baby, that you shouldn't expect to do anything in your life other than comfort and care for that baby. If you don't expect to do anything else, then you won't feel frustrated because you haven't done it.

The crying doesn't last forever so let other people do as much as they can. Your priority is looking after yourself and your child.'

Re-establishing the couple relationship

The emotional toll from living with a crying baby can be quite overwhelming. With your nerves constantly on edge and your self-confidence undermined, it is no wonder that many mothers of crying babies become depressed and take out their frustration on their partner. Often anger that cannot be expressed towards the baby is directed towards the partner.

Marianne remembers vividly how it felt:

'It just went on and on, night after night, and I thought that it would never end. It destroyed any self-confidence I'd ever had as a mother. And because I couldn't take it out on the baby, I took it out on Jonathan. Anything he did wasn't good enough, wasn't the way I would have done it.'

Delia and Graham's baby, Guy, had unremitting colic until he was five months old, and then developed into an unhappy, demanding, unpredictable baby who, as Graham admits, was 'very difficult to love'. Looking back now, he is amazed that his relationship with Delia survived:

'We would judge each other, blame each other. Nothing either of us did was right. It had to be the other one's fault. We had no time together when Guy wasn't crying, it seems, for the whole of that first year. It was very hard to hold onto the people we had been . . . and we nearly didn't.'

Carmel and her partner, James, felt that their daughter Abby's continued crying was a problem they had to tackle together:

'We went to see the doctor because we were a family in crisis. I felt horrible – James couldn't do anything right despite the fact that he was doing as much as he could. He was often late for work and tried to come home early to help out, and was living under the pressure I was putting on him to do more. James and I felt we had no relationship to speak of, just an awareness that there had once been one and that somewhere underneath all this tension and exhaustion we were still the same two people.'

Susan and Keith also worked together to cope with their baby's crying, but the strain on the relationship soon showed:

'I was very low for a long, long time. I'd be in tears most days when Keith came home and Simon would be on my lap grizzling if it was a good day, shrieking if it was a bad one. Neither of us had ever encountered anything like this before and it was tough on both of us, but Keith had to draw on all his reserves to support me. The crying wore into our time together and wore any closeness away. Keith did everything he could to make things better and I took and took, but I still also took my frustration and resentment out on him. I had to. There was no other emotional release. And even while I was doing it, knowing I was doing it, I couldn't escape this unpleasant feeling that the marriage was over and wondering what state benefits I would have to rely on as a single parent.'   *Susan*

Carmel, too, felt that she and James came close to splitting up:

'We were so horrible to one another, blaming each other, that I sometimes thought that we'd never be able to talk to one another like rational human beings again.'

When Carmel was diagnosed with postnatal depression, she felt that this helped:

'Once the suffering had a label, it was easier to place a perspective on it. James and I began to see how things had gradually deteriorated and things could improve.'

If, as a couple, you are able to give each other some 'time off', that will help you to cope with the crying. What it won't do is give you some time together, away from the screams and the misery, and that is what we all need to keep us sane and to re-establish our closeness as a couple. Paula enlisted family help:

> 'One evening a week, my mother came round and took over while we went out for a drink. It didn't matter whether Kirsten was screaming. My mum said she was used to it because I'd been just the same!'

When you've just given birth, it is easy to become absorbed by the baby's demands and even if you want to spend time alone with your partner, you may find it impossible:

> 'We think Daisy had some sort of inbuilt radar device. If we attempted so much as a quick peck on the cheek, we'd immediately hear her stirring and starting to cry.'
> *Mary*

Maria found that in her quest to keep up with her son George's demands, she had no time for her partner:

> 'To be honest, I had no inclination for sex whatsoever. My breasts leaked, my eyes were closing with tiredness . . . If Peter even tried to give me a cuddle, I just pushed him away.'

One thing that will help is talking honestly and openly to your partner about how you feel. If you feel that the pressure to have sex is more than you can cope with when you're worn out coping with your crying baby, then you must say so, rather than let further anger and resentment build up.

'I felt John was using "work" as an escape route. If the crying got too much, he could walk out the door, stay late at the office. I know it was hard to come home to this unhappy house, but I hated him for leaving me trapped in it.'   *Kerry*

Many fathers of crying babies feel just as helpless and rejected by the baby as mothers do and can come to resent this little creature who has disrupted the partnership. Again, if you can make it clear to your partner that there are ways in which he can help, and that this is a problem you can solve together, this may defuse some of the tension.

Difficult days

Most couples experience some difficulties in their relationship during the baby and child-rearing days. It's to be expected. It's even more to be expected when there is a crying baby to cope with, too. Don't add to your stress by believing that everyone else is supremely happy and you're the only ones arguing.

A crying baby is hardest to cope with when you are alone. If you and your partner can give each other mutual support rather than let the continued crying drive you further apart, the burden of isolation won't seem so great. Every new parent needs to spend time with other adults, not just the baby, to define their sense of self, to re-establish their identity as they adjust to the new role of 'parent', and this is where partners can be of great help.

For single parents, finding mutual support with other single parents can be a lifeline. There are several organisations listed on page 152 which you can use as a starting point, and ask your health visitor to put you in touch with other lone parents in the local area. Katherine and Gail, who were both living alone, developed a very practical support system for each other:

'One day I'd do my shopping while Gail had the boys, then the next day she'd go. If either one of us felt it was becoming too much – and this often used to happen at the end of the day, round about 6pm when we were all worn out – we could go round to the other's, hand over the baby for an hour and just get some respite. Sometimes it meant that one of us had two yelling babies in the house, but it was just as noisy with one. And as the boys got older, they became good friends.'   *Katherine*

Long-term exhaustion

If your baby's crying has gone on for several weeks or months, you will feel worn down, tired and depressed:

'Of course I became depressed. Who wouldn't when they're living day after day with a child who is so unhappy that they're always crying?'   *Amy*

Constant crying is also extremely demoralising:

> 'The days were lonely and terribly long. I felt com-
> pletely inadequate, a social outcast and, most of all,
> lonely. The lowest point came when my partner
> found me weeping into Joshua's breakfast, unable to
> face another day.'   *Alex*

> 'It was torture. We loved Maeve so very much but it
> seemed like she hated us.'   *Siobhan*

Quite often mothers put the blame on themselves for
their baby's continued crying, believing that it is due to
some inadequacy in themselves or their parenting:

> 'It was easy to blame myself. After all, Georgia was
> crying so I must be a bad mother.'   *Michele*

> 'Nothing I did seemed to help. I used to end up
> crying myself, trying to get Caroline to stop crying,
> all the time feeling how useless I was, how pathetic.'
>   *Marianne*

Research shows that persistent crying in the early months
is unlikely due to inadequate parenting. Knowing this may
help, because it means that you shouldn't take the crying
'personally', as if it's all down to you. In a recent study, the
parents of babies who cried excessively were notable for
their high levels of care.

Even knowing that it's not our fault won't always
stop us blaming ourselves, however. Gina, whose baby

Ellen cried more or less constantly, remembers this only too well:

> 'Ellen cried all the time, day and night, as a baby. She didn't sleep through the night until she was three and during the day she was never contented. I convinced myself that if I kept responding to her every need, even when it was hard to work out what those needs were, I would eventually be able to make her happy. But it just went on and on and I was so exhausted and worn down that I just let it go on and on.'

Mary, too, constantly looked for explanations in her own behaviour:

> 'Had I tired Daisy out that day by taking her to the shops in the sling? Perhaps it was because I had eaten some spicy soup and she didn't like the taste of it in my breast milk? Or maybe I wasn't feeding her enough? All the time, I was trying to second-guess myself.'

Perhaps because of this underlying suspicion that it is our fault, many of us find it hard to let anyone else know how difficult life has become. We bottle up our feelings and this adds to the stress. This is what Maria found:

> 'I was so guilty all the time. I didn't play with him enough. I didn't love him enough. In my imagination had been an image of myself as the most kind,

loving, "perfect" mother, and here I was failing on every level. How could I tell anyone that?'

'I thought I might be making a fuss over nothing. I decided it must just be me. Other mothers coped.'

Carla

Michele feels that one of the most important things is to 'tell someone':

'If your baby cries a lot, it is easy to assume that you are doing something wrong, so you keep the problem a secret. Don't. Share the burden. Let someone know you are having a rough time.'

Naomi had an unusual pattern of crying with her son, Jacob:

'He was my middle child and, unlike the other two, screamed . . . but only at mealtimes. From the age of six months until he was about one, mealtimes with Jacob were ear-splitting. When I met another person who had a similar problem, it helped enormously. I wasn't the only "freak"!'

When it all gets too much

Most of us love our babies immediately, and this can make those early days bearable. Carmel, on the other hand, found the opposite:

'I felt very little for Abby, as if she wasn't a real person at all. In some ways that made those first few weeks of hell that bit easier. I remember a woman at work saying to me, years ago, that it took six weeks to fall in love with your baby, but the six weeks came and went and no lightning flash, no thunderbolt, nothing. It was as the crying went on and on and I felt I was starting to lose any link with this baby, that I knew I needed help.'

Yet even if we fall in love with our babies instantly, that love can be severely tested. Cathy remembers how, under the strain of caring for Natalie, who needed constant holding, she became emotionally detached:

'People would tell me how beautiful she was, and I would feel pleased that they felt that way, but I was unable to see it for myself.'

Veronica remembers how this feeling of distance crept in:

'I tried to be part of the mother-and-toddler circuit but somehow felt outside the role. The biggest feeling was one of loss. The person I had been – capable, intelligent, lively, busy – was gone and had been replaced by someone incapable, cramped and boring. I wanted to be free to walk at my own pace, discuss something other than teething. I didn't have a mind to fit my life. I couldn't see how to get me back while still being a mum, which brought me into direct conflict with myself.'

This emotional distance can have distorting effects on the mind, as well. Marianne couldn't get rid of a lingering irrational fear:

'I became convinced that they'd given me someone else's child. People kept saying it would get better but I was equally sure it wouldn't because I knew that Caroline was crying because she knew I wasn't her real mum.'

Some of us find our cranky, colicky, constantly crying baby extremely difficult to love, and this can make caring for the baby almost intolerable:

'I used to ask my husband whether it was too late to take him back and say we'd decided to give him up for adoption. And I was only half-joking.' *Rosa*

Paula also found Kirsten difficult to love:

'How could I love her when she so plainly hated me? Most of the first month of her life, I had no feelings whatsoever towards her. I just regarded her as a nuisance that it was my lot to look after and I was bitterly resentful.'

Maria noticed how her feelings gradually changed as the crying continued:

'When George was born, I had loved him instantly, with a passion. They had laid him on my tummy seconds after his birth and I just gazed in wonder at this tiny creature. It was as days and weeks and months went by and the crying didn't stop that I began to hate him. Even now it's hard to admit that, but I did.'

No one can really tell you beforehand what it might feel like to be woken up by a crying baby for the fifth or sixth time that night. It can feel like sustained torture. When crying persists, therefore, it is not surprising that many parents become angry or hostile towards the baby, as Alex began to understand:

'All I can remember of the first six months of Joshua's life is the sheer misery of it all. He cried endlessly for no apparent reason. Joshua particularly hated his expensive pram, his Moses basket, walks in the countryside, trips to the supermarket . . . In fact, he seemed to hate everything, most of all me. I sometimes hated him, too. For the first time in my life I could understand how people could shake or hurt their baby in a rage.'

If the crying becomes overwhelming, acknowledge this and act upon this feeling. Give the baby to someone else to hold, put him in his Moses basket or cot and leave the room, tell yourself that you have done all you can for now and give yourself five or ten minutes away from the crying. If you learned relaxation techniques to help you cope with labour, put them to use now.

Some parents, driven to distraction, worry that they will harm their baby in a sudden snap of temper:

'You will not be alone if your baby makes you feel very angry. You will not be the first mother to contemplate shaking, slapping or even killing a crying baby. I used to wish an "accident" on Georgia so that she would have to go to hospital and someone would take her off me for a while. When she did eventually sleep, I used to wish she would die a cot death. I did shake her at one point and can see why parents are driven to harming their children at times like this.'

Michele

Amy, too, recalls how she reached breaking point:

'I'd had enough. I lifted him up and shook him, even though I knew it was pointless, I was just so angry that he wasn't responding to all of my efforts. I'd reached the end of my patience.'

Even shaking a baby can cause her damage. Amy knew this, yet it still didn't stop her when the crying became unendurable and she lost control. If you feel an urge to hurt your child, as many parents do, put your baby down somewhere safe and walk away. She will come to much less harm if you leave her alone, preferably out of hearing range, for ten minutes while you calm down and regain control, than if you let yourself get pushed over the edge.

'I came close to losing my temper often. I think the only thing that stopped me was that in the back of my mind I knew it would help no one.'

Majella

Take your anger and frustration out somewhere else – throw some cushions about, pummel the sofa, walk around the garden. It's also worth contacting the telephone helplines (see page 143) where people will understand just what you're going through. This will help to deal with the immediate crisis.

Once you are calm again, however, you need to take some action to help you cope in the long term. It will do neither you nor your baby any good if you let yourself be constantly driven to breaking point. There is no single solution that will help every baby or every family, but sharing the problem is one of the most important things you can do to make things better:

> 'Being a parent is hard work. Being a parent of a crying baby is exceptionally hard work. You need to find someone who will understand your feelings of aggression towards your baby and not condemn you for them.' *Michele*

Your health visitor can help you devise ways to cope with your own particular situation and may be able to put you in touch with local support groups. Your GP may recommend a counsellor. For Maria, voicing her true worries to her partner was of help:

> 'One night, when George was about eight months old, I was lying next to Peter in the dark, unable to go to sleep because I knew the crying would soon start up again, and I finally said what had been on my mind for days and days: "What if it's always like

this? What if I never love him? What if he doesn't love me?" Just hearing myself say it was a release. Of course Peter did his best to reassure me and, although I wasn't convinced, I felt better now that he knew just how deep my worries went.'

It is often only when we do manage to break that vicious circle of crying, anger and guilt that things can begin to get better:

'On the first night after we had both got a decent night's sleep, unbroken by the crying and screams that had gone on for so long, Kirsten woke up and smiled at me. She was a different child. I was over-whelmed with first relief, and then love. I felt I had had a glimpse of the "true" Kirsten and, even if things did go downhill and she became unhappy again, at least I would have a sense of the real person in there that I was dealing with, not just a noisy, tiresome monster.'   *Paula*

It may also help to remind yourself that while crying lasts on average for about three months, many parents experi-ence an emotional dip at around six weeks. This may be partly due to the fact that, consciously or not, both parents feel that things somehow ought to have got back to 'normal' by now, or the mother is putting pressure on herself to get into a 'routine' before returning to work after maternity leave. Being aware that this is an emotional low point may help you to ask for extra emotional and practical support at this crucial time.

4

Survival strategies

When you're pacing the bedroom with a heavy head tucked into your shoulder and your baby's crying reverberating in your ears, is there anything you can do, anything at all that will help?

Over the centuries, hundreds of methods of calming a crying baby have been road-tested by harassed parents. The inescapable conclusion seems to be that what will work for one baby (or parent) won't work for another.

In this chapter, then, we've rounded up some of the most promising strategies that have worked for parents in the past. Some of them you will have heard before because if there's one thing you're never short of as the parent of a crying baby, it's advice. Advice can be welcome or unwelcome, asked for or delivered anyway, regardless of your feelings, and much of the advice will be completely contradictory ('Feed her more', 'Feed her less'). If you followed every single piece of advice, both you and your baby would end up confused. Yet we include here techniques that have worked for other parents and which you can choose whether or not to try.

You will notice that some are completely contradictory but they're both in there because they have both worked for different babies.

Through trial and error, you may find a way that will soothe your baby and feel right for your family. Keeping in mind that your baby is an individual with her own personal preferences can help put things in perspective:

> 'Don't expect your baby to be like the ones in the books, on TV, or even similar to those of your friends. If your baby won't lie in a crib, sit in a chair and sleep in the pram, grit your teeth and find out what does work. In my case, I carried Georgia around on my shoulder for three months.' *Michele*

If a suggestion doesn't feel right for you, don't try it: you have to be completely confident about what you are doing, otherwise it is likely that your baby will pick up on your stress and anxiety . . . and cry all the more. Remember that these strategies can work both ways: if they make you feel better, you will be more able to cope with your baby's crying; if they help your baby to settle, you will feel better, too.

If you do decide to give something a go, give it time to work. The one thing that everyone agrees on with crying babies is that there is no miracle cure; nothing will happen instantly. However, with calm and perseverance, you may find that one of these techniques calms you, or your baby, or both of you.

Swaddling

This is an age-old method for calming babies and is especially effective with new-borns, perhaps because it reminds them of the security of the womb.

❑ Put your baby on a soft cotton sheet.
❑ Fold one side of the sheet over your baby and tuck it over her arm and underneath her.
❑ Fold the other side across the other way and tuck it in under her body.
❑ Now you have a little bundle with her arms wrapped snugly next to her body.

Of course, some babies will enjoy the complete opposite and will be very happy if you stay with them for ten minutes or so at each nappy change, just letting them kick unhindered on the mat.

Slings and other baby carriers

Many babies simply like to be held . . . a lot.

> 'All my babies liked to be cuddled closely and firmly. Gentle stroking across the scalp from front to back was also very soothing.'   *Debra*

Some babies like to be held close to the chest – perhaps

because the sound of the parent's heartbeat is reassuring; some prefer to be held more upright, near your shoulder.

Many parents have found that slings soothe their baby and help to reduce the crying in a way that nothing else can. Perhaps it is the sense of being held securely and firmly close to their parent, the sound of their heartbeat, the rocking as their parent walks about . . . or a combination of all three.

The design of baby carriers varies widely and there are several types:

❑ *Front-carriers*. Most are suitable for new-borns onwards, although some designs mean that a new-born will need additional head support. These can provide a great deal of reassurance for your baby as she is held very close to you.
❑ *Slings*. These are a modern version of the old idea of tying your baby to you with a blanket. They allow your baby to be carried in a variety of positions, usually off to the side.
❑ *Back-carriers*. These are sturdy and safe and give you more freedom of movement, but can only be used once your baby can sit unsupported.

You may like to borrow a sling or carrier first, to see if its design suits you and your baby. You will need to be comfortable, so it's worth checking that the fasteners won't press into your particular body just at the wrong point, for example. Before you buy one, make sure you can fasten all the straps or cope with the buckles on your own. A design that means you have to have someone else to fasten the baby in, for example, won't be much use if you're alone a lot of the time.

Michele found that a sling worked for her:

> 'Being upright and close to her mother was what Georgia needed, and I used the sling all day if need be. I did the washing up with her in the sling, talked on the phone, went to the loo, watched *Richard and Judy* . . . '

Others find that while a sling doesn't stop the baby crying, putting him in one can free the parent's hands to get on with other tasks like peeling potatoes, shopping, vacuuming . . . This fact alone can stop parents feeling so trapped and resentful of the crying:

> 'I became extremely adept at cooking, washing and, at a push, doing the ironing, while carrying baby in a sling.'   *Jane*

Safety first

Like anything you buy for your baby, make sure that any baby carrier you use comes from a reputable manufacturer and conforms to British safety standards. Safety is always a priority when transporting babies, even if it's just transporting them round the house.

Yvonne found a sling useful for another reason:

> 'When I'd left Lois to cry it out, I'd worry and worry all the time she was crying. Then when she stopped crying I'd worry as well, in case she had strangled herself or something. In the sling, I always knew she was safe, even if she was having a misery bout.'

Rocking

One of the attractions of a sling is the gentle rocking rhythm the baby experiences while being carried about. This is part of its attraction for a baby. There are also special 'baby swings' about and automated rocking devices which can save your arms if your baby enjoys these. When the baby is a little older, some parents find that a baby bouncer gives them respite from the crying for long enough to gets a few jobs done as Amy found:

> 'Duncan cried not because he was an unhappy baby but because he was a bored baby. A few minutes in the baby bouncer would keep him entertained and give me long enough to do some really simple task like pegging the laundry out or changing the bed. It gave us both a break.'

Colette had a rocking chair; she often fed William in this, then soothed him to sleep by rocking back and forth afterwards:

'It felt a very natural thing to do. It calmed me down and I got much less agitated about his crying. He also liked being patted on the back.'

Bed sharing

Many parents find that the baby who cries and cries at night miraculously stops crying if brought into the warmth and comfort of the family bed, although this is not recommended if either of the parents smoke. Debra found that this worked well for Angus, her fifth child, although there were some disadvantages:

'Angus breastfed whilst I slept and was happiest in our bed. He only cried at night if we tried to put him into his own cot. However, he still (aged three) sleeps in our bed every night and breastfeeds every morning. It gets more and more difficult for me and my husband, regularly sharing a bed with two children (Angus is very restless) so the prevention of the crying nights has had long-term consequences for our sleep . . . and for our love-making.'

Being in close human contact is a real need for 'clingy' babies and you may find that your baby's crying is dramatically reduced if she has the reassurance of you next to her all night. Sleeping with your baby may also help your own exhaustion:

'I decided to take Caitlin into bed with me to feed and almost immediately fell asleep. I couldn't tell you how many times that night she woke for a feed because I dozed or slept through most of it. In the morning I felt so much more rested than on the nights when I'd been walking her up and down the bedroom floor, it was like a miracle. It also made me feel much closer to her. It was the key to our survival.'
Penny

Yvonne worried at first what bringing the baby into bed would do for her relationship with her partner:

'I worried that Tony would see it as one more intrusion of the baby into our lives, as if we would never get any peace. But once he found that his sleep was broken less, not more, once Lois was in our bed, it worked well. And instead of spending the nights worrying about the baby because she was crying and worrying about Tony because his sleep was being broken and he had to work the next day, the burden was lifted.'

Tanya, too, found that bed-sharing gave her a whole new dimension on parenting:

'Once Evan was in with us, I felt more rested and during the days I actually began to enjoy him, instead of looking on him as this thing which needed feeding or being rocked to sleep all the time.'

Sedatives

Several of the women I spoke to had either been prescribed sedatives for their baby or had bought an over-the-counter medicine which induced drowsiness as a side-effect. While most of us know instinctively that it is not the best approach to parenting to drug our babies into a chemically induced slumber, it is something that many of us contemplate as we reach the end of our tether. This is not a new practice; parents down the centuries have been giving their fretful infants a small nip of brandy or equivalent to lull them off to sleep, and old recipes for gripe water are remarkable for their alcoholic content.

Babies are teetotal

Giving your baby even a teaspoon of alcohol to help her sleep is dangerous. Even tiny amounts can overload her digestive system and make her unwell.

We decided that, in a book like this, we had to acknowledge the fact that many parents do occasionally use sedatives to guarantee themselves and their baby one peaceful night, although the effects of different medications, and potentially damaging side-effects, can vary from baby to baby. Polly was one of the unlucky ones:

'We'd tried all the usual remedies, including leaving him to cry, dosing him with Phenergan, going back every five minutes, none of which worked. Finally, I pleaded with my GP who prescribed five days' worth of a sleeping drug to give us all a break. It had the opposite effect. Unfortunately, Jamie was one of the small proportion of children who become hyperactive on this medicine. It was almost the final straw.'

Indeed, some parents find that the drugs have no noticeable effect on the sleeping or crying problem. Some can even slow intestinal activity and cause more wind and constipation, making the crying worse. If this is something you are thinking about, then talk to your health visitor or GP. That way you know that whatever you are prescribed is safe for your baby to take. Do not risk your baby's health with anything else. Many sleeping drugs are not licensed to be given to young children and even if you *are* prescribed one as a short-term measure, it will not solve your problem in the long term.

Driving

As many parents will testify, taking a screaming baby out in the car or the pram is an occupation not necessarily confined to the daylight hours:

'We relied on driving Alice round in the car to get her off to sleep. Fortunately, she could be unstrapped and lifted from the car to the house without waking.'

Kate

'If you go for a drive in the middle of the night, the baby may stop crying, but if she doesn't you will be concentrating on the road and the crying doesn't seem so annoying.'

Michele

Of course, driving has the opposite effect on some babies, and they go into a frenzy every time they see the car seat. If you have to drive somewhere, says Cathy, and your baby yells:

'Open all the windows and the crying doesn't seem so loud.'

Jane found that the only way to accomplish the half-hour car drive to the nearest town was if her partner drove and she breastfed continuously throughout the journey, though this is not without safety risks.

Dummies, thumbs and fingers

Many babies have a pronounced need to suck. You can offer the breast – for comfort rather than nutrition – or a (clean) finger or a dummy. Kate noticed this with Alice:

'Eating was either done in shifts or, if I was on my own, I would sit her in her car seat beside me and let her suck on my little finger while I ate with the other hand.'

Many parents, even if they were certain before the baby's arrival that they would never use a dummy, change their minds when faced with the reality of having to placate a baby who won't stop crying.

'I thought dummies were extremely nasty. They were unhygienic, unattractive, and seeing a baby with this big bit of plastic stuck in their mouth seemed such a shame, somehow. Duncan didn't need a dummy, breastfeeding was all he seemed to need, and I was pleased about that. But I changed my mind remarkably quickly when it came to Celine. She didn't have a loud cry, just insistent and oppressive, especially when I was busy doing something for Duncan like getting his breakfast. A dummy seemed like a miracle. She didn't need me necessarily, I worked out, but she needed to suck something. If it kept her happy, which it did, then why should I make us all miserable by not letting her have one because I didn't like the look of it?'   *Amy*

Maria also found that a dummy helped:

'Once George had (finally) fallen asleep, we used to find that he was woken by wind, sometimes only a few minutes later. And then the edge would have been taken off his need for sleep and he'd be awake and cross and crying until the next feed. If he fell asleep with a dummy, when he became slightly disturbed I'd watch him suck on that and it seemed to get him over the hurdle and back into a deep sleep without waking fully. Once he began having more regular deep sleeps, the crying began to abate.'

Most experts agree that, if used in moderation throughout the first year, dummies are not something to worry about. It is only with prolonged use against developing teeth when the child is older that speech and dental problems with misalignment of the teeth can occur. And this is where dummies are not without their drawbacks, however:

'When she took a dummy, I just sobbed with relief. Unfortunately the knock-on effect of the heavy reliance on a dummy is that Alice is still addicted to it at seven years old.'   *Kate*

Dara feels that she met Ben's need to suck in the wrong way:

'It was fine at first. He slept in our bed and when he cried I fed him. But when he moved to a cot at 18 months, I decided it was time for the night feeds to stop as he didn't really need milk halfway through the night any more and, after a year and a half of not having one single night without disturbance, I was permanently shattered. But Ben had other ideas. He woke frequently, would not take a dummy, would not take water, screamed and sobbed and drove me to my wits' end. I found a solution in giving him juice in a bottle. In the middle of the night, you will do anything, anything just to get some sleep. I started this as a short-term measure but it soon became a habit like any other and I was alarmed by how quickly the dental decay began. So another battle began, which was only solved after many more months of broken sleep.'

Never dip dummies into anything sweet. It isn't just the amount of sugar that causes dental decay, but how long it remains in the mouth. Even if your baby doesn't have teeth when you start this practice, he will have them before long, so it's a habit that's best not started.

Some children, by luck or by accident, find their thumbs at around four weeks of age, and this method of comforting themselves can be equally rewarding or equally irritating, depending on the views of the parent. Unlike a dummy, thumbs can't be taken away when the child is older, but as a society we seem to be getting less worried about these small comfort mechanisms. At the first hint of stress or strain, my daughter, at six, will plunge her thumb in her mouth. I have decided that it is not a problem for me (no matter what relatives say) and I am sure that the instant it becomes a problem for her, she will do something about it.

What you do need to watch out for, if you are a breastfeeding mother who decides to use a dummy, is that you balance your baby's need for comfort-sucking against her need to suckle at the breast to stimulate your milk supply. This is especially important when your baby is going through a growth spurt and needs to feed more often than usual.

Crying it out

Helen remembers the day she was at the end of her tether:

> 'I'd tried everything. I'd walked her, patted her, rocked her, and in the end, I was so exhausted that I just put her down in her Moses basket, inside the cot, and left her to cry it out. That first time, it must have taken five, six minutes, that's all. Then it all went quiet. Of course, I ran up the stairs – as quietly as I could – and Bethany was actually asleep. I wondered whether I'd simply been keeping her awake with all this activity.'

Gina discovered that this sometimes worked with Ellen, too:

> 'As long as I was happy that I'd done my best to meet all her needs, I felt that she sometimes needed to cry it out. I noticed she especially cried when she was tired because she just couldn't put herself to sleep easily and often needed to cry herself into sleep.'

Bathtime

Warm water has a soothing effect on many adults, so, not surprisingly, it does on some babies, too. As part of a regular night-time routine, it can calm the baby and alert her that bedtime is coming up.

> 'A regular routine, established early, definitely helped mine to learn that bedtime was bedtime. It was reassuring to us all.'   *Debra*

A bath, either with you or in her baby bath, is a trusted and often-used measure to signal to the baby on a regular basis that the day is over and the night has begun. Its relaxation benefits can be emphasised if you combine it with a calm massage before bed. Like everything else, don't expect your baby to get the message instantly. The familiarity of the routine, which comes when it is used day after day, is an important part of the learning process.

Massage

Before birth, babies are constantly rocked, soothed and nurtured. After they are born, most babies respond well to continued close contact with their parents. Massage is one way to continue this contact as the baby responds both physiologically and emotionally to your touch. Massage stimulates the lymphatic and circulatory systems, and also gives parents confidence in handling their baby and allows non-verbal communication, which is sometimes all we can manage!

While massage won't always bring about an instant cure for a crying baby (I have seen one baby – mine – cry all the way through a massage), massage can have the long-term effect of soothing and relaxing a baby. If she has a massage that afternoon, she may sleep more soundly that night. Or it may have unexpected benefits, as Sandra found out:

> 'I'd expected Callum to be more relaxed, possibly drowsy. Instead, he was actually more alert than usual, looking over my shoulder and taking notice of his surroundings. This was unusual. He was generally too busy crying to take much notice of anything.'

Don't feel, either, that you have to turn to a 'professional' for a massage, although many mother-and-baby groups will often invite someone to demonstrate the basic techniques. Massage relaxes the body naturally and is a natural skill. As long as your baby is fit and well, you can try simple massage at home. An ideal time is following the bath, just before bedtime or naptime. You don't need to use a massage oil but it is probably easier if you do, especially if your baby has dry skin. Almond oil is smooth, light and sweet-smelling.

The basics are as follows:

❑ Massage your baby in a warm room.
❑ Put a teaspoon or two of the oil into a saucer.
❑ Wash your hands and warm them.

- ❏ Undress your baby and place her on a towel, facing you.
- ❏ Rub a few drops of oil into your hands to warm the oil.
- ❏ Massage your baby using a light, circular motion, and a light, gentle touch. You may like to begin with circular movements clockwise across the abdomen, which allows eye-to-eye contact.
- ❏ Then try what your hands and instinct tell you to do: gentle stroking along the arms and legs, kneading of the thighs and calves, and firm but gentle hand movements across the back.
- ❏ You may like to try singing to your baby while massaging.

Massage can be as relaxing and stress-reducing for the parent as it is for the baby, but it will only work if you respond to your baby's signals. If she becomes distressed (many babies dislike being naked for too long, for example) or unresponsive, stop and try again another day. Don't forget that a massage for you, too, might be a good idea!

If you're interested in learning more about massage, many GP practices and baby clinics have advertisements on the noticeboard for baby massage courses and there are some introductory videos available. These can tell you more about the techniques involved.

Never use 'essential' or aromatherapy oils on any baby under three months without expert advice. Even after that time they should only be used with care and caution.

Music

Many babies find music soothing. The music itself doesn't have to be soothing and you may get just as good a result with the latest Number One as Beethoven. On the whole, however, babies prefer melodic tunes and quite a few mothers believe they show a preference for music they heard in the womb. Claire listened to a lot of Mozart while she was expecting Jenna:

'After she was born she definitely seemed to become calmer if I played the same music. She didn't become more relaxed, in fact she became more alert, but all round less sad.'

Carla found that 90-minute tapes that she'd filled with music especially useful when her baby cried:

'Most fits of crying were over before the 90-minute tape finished. When it's just you and the baby, it feels like the screaming has been going on forever. The music helped me to calm down and also helped me to time the crying, either to prove that I was right and it really was going on for as long as I said it did, or there were some days when I realised it wasn't as bad as before.'

Perhaps the most soothing music a baby can hear, however, is her parents' own voices. No doubt this is why many lullabies are so old: they have been passed down from generation to generation as a tried and trusted method of getting babies to sleep. Amazingly, it doesn't seem to matter how off-key the singing is.

> 'I sang to both of mine. It was astonishing how many old songs I found I knew. And Christmas carols I thought I'd forgotten. It was useful distraction therapy for me, as well, on the nights when they were hard to settle.'
>
> *Amy*

Noise

Not all babies require music to calm themselves. For some, any old noise will do, as long it's reasonably loud, repetitive and monotonous. Hence vacuum cleaners and washing machines lull them off to sleep . . . or their father's snoring. This is easy to understand: they've spent a long time in their mother's womb, which isn't the quietest place in the world, and a sudden silence may be quite disconcerting.

'The only thing that soothed Ruth was the noise of the Hoover. Unfortunately, as we lived in a flat, I couldn't have the Hoover on for hours every day. So I made an hour-long tape of the Hoover, put that next to her cot, and she drifted off to it peacefully for the first four or five months of her life.'   *Faye*

Carol made her discovery by accident:

'I had had a bath and washed my hair, all to the sound of Mark's crying, but when I switched on the hairdryer (partly hoping to drown out the noise) I found that he instantly stopped crying. He was hypnotised by the constant drone of the background noise and soon fell asleep. This worked for my second baby (also a crying baby) too.'

Some parents find that their babies are soothed if their basket or baby-seat is put near the washing machine or dryer. The combination of the noise, warmth and vibration seems to have a calming effect. DO NOT put your baby on top of any item of household equipment, however! The dangers of leaving the baby unattended are too great.

Some parents find 'white noise' or 'womb music' tapes useful – they simulate the sound of the mother's womb and can be most effective if introduced before six weeks of age.

'A baby soother tape was a wonderful discovery. It would keep Maeve asleep for 30 minutes. An hour if I rushed upstairs and turned the tape over quickly.'
Siobhan

Jenny, on the other hand, found that her baby, Susanne, settled more easily in a room with dark, peace and quiet! As with everything, it is a question of adapting your approach to your baby's sensitivities.

Homoeopathy

Homoeopathy uses extracts of natural plants and mineral substances in a very, very diluted form with the aim of promoting the body's natural healing ability. Its main principle is to treat 'like with like'. This means, paradoxically, that a remedy is chosen on the basis that in large quantities it can produce symptoms similar to those that the person is experiencing. The amounts used in treatment, however, are so minute and diluted, that it is hard to see how they can have any effect. Yet they do.

As with all complementary therapies, homoeopathy is a holistic treatment. That means that it treats the whole person – their character, background, experience and reactions – and not just a particular set of symptoms. One crying baby may well be offered a different remedy to another. Polly – whose son, Jamie, at ten months old was still waking up crying several times a night – was initially not convinced:

'I saw an advert in our local newsletter and by this stage desperation had overtaken everything else, so I called the number. At our first consultation, I immediately felt more confident. It lasted an hour, and never before had anyone (GP, midwife, health visitor) taken so much interest in Jamie as a person. I was asked about the pregnancy, the labour and birth, his vaccinations and how he reacted, his likes and dislikes . . . and only after we had gone through all this information was I prescribed a remedy. The homoeopath decided to treat Jamie with sulphur. At first, Jamie seemed more wakeful than ever, and very ebullient and energetic, but after a couple of days he 'came down' from this. Improvement was slow. I'd say that after one week he was waking once or twice a night, and things gradually got better. Since then, we've been for regular reviews and homoeopathy is now something I'd choose to treat all of us.'

Many parents find that homoeopathic remedies have a beneficial effect on their babies, but they must be used with caution. They are not generally recommended for babies under three months old and even after that time should be used with care and control. Always seek the advice of an expert.

If you have a baby who cries constantly and are interested in this form of treatment, consult a homoeopath for specialised advice on the remedy most appropriate for your baby.

Homoeopathy has gained more and more credibility with the medical establishment over recent years and there are now many GPs who practise homoeopathy alongside conventional medicine. There are also several NHS hospitals where you can receive homoeopathic treatment, for example, in Bristol, London, Glasgow and Liverpool.

Herbal remedies

Herbal remedies make use of plant extracts to form preparations that are usually gentle, with fewer side-effects than mainstream drugs.

John, who had found herbal remedies of benefit to himself in the past, felt that this was a natural avenue to explore when his son, Ivan, showed all the classic symptoms of 'colic':

'I simply went along and spoke to the person who'd made up remedies for me before, explained Ivan's symptoms, and they made something up for me to try. It did seem to help, although whether that was because I was convinced it would help, and therefore immediately became less tense about the evening to come, and Ivan responded to my more relaxed state, I don't know. But for whatever reason it helped, it did help. Not instantly, and the colic didn't completely disappear until Ivan was near three months, but I felt it did alleviate the pain. And the hours of crying gradually lessened.'

Aromatherapy

Aromatherapy makes use of the therapeutic properties of 'essential oils' which are extracted from flowers, grasses, roots, leaves and trees. Julie, whose son Toby developed a difficulty in settling at night when he was around a year old, found that lavender oil helped:

> 'I used to put a single drop of lavender oil, mixed with a few teaspoons of almond oil, in his bath-water. It certainly made him much calmer and ready for sleep.'

Robert also felt that lavender helped his son Connor to settle (eventually) to sleep, although his method was different:

> 'I'd put one drop of oil in one or two pints of boiled water in a bowl. I'd put the bowl on the floor, well away from the cot. As the steam rose, you could feel this soothing scent permeating the bedroom. The effect was undeniable. You could see Connor relax.'

If you want to try using essential oils, always remember the following – and this applies to adults just as much as children:

❑ They should always be used diluted well in a 'carrier' oil or water.
❑ They must never be applied neat to the skin.
❑ They are not meant to be taken internally.

Aromatherapy, or burning essential oils, can certainly calm a parent, and this worked for Andrea:

'When Tyler woke in the middle of the night for a feed, he was often agitated and took a long time to settle at the breast. So I used to leave him in his cot for a minute while I put a couple of drops of oil on the burner, and it calmed me to have the room fill with mandarin fragrance, or the scent of camomile, and because I was calm, he calmed more easily, too.'

A recipe for relaxation

You will need:

- ❏ a calming essential oil like lavender
- ❏ water
- ❏ a diffuser with a candle.

Add one drop of your chosen essential oil to a dessertspoon of water and mix well. Add a little of this water to the cupped area of the diffuser. Light the candle and relax.

Many aromatherapists combine the use of essential oils with the art of massage. With all complementary therapies, always consult someone fully qualified. Not all oils are recommended for use with young babies and you will need advice. Details of how to find a registered aromatherapist in your area are given on page 146.

Cranial osteopathy

The bones in a baby's skull have not yet completely fused together at the time of birth, allowing for small tolerances in movement which help the baby's head to adapt to the forces of labour and the passage down the birth canal. In addition, if the baby has been subjected to extra complications, such as a forceps or ventouse delivery, then the skull may become distorted further.

Osteopaths believe that they can treat these distortions with gentle massage and manipulation of the baby's head, bringing everything back into proper alignment, relieving the stresses and strains, and thus helping the baby to develop naturally. This technique is known as cranial osteopathy.

Cranial osteopathy is a technique that many parents have found to help with such diverse problems as feeding difficulties, disturbed sleep patterns, colic and crying. It is becoming increasingly popular. Nicole feels that it certainly helped her:

'Emily was delivered by forceps after a very long and drawn-out labour. After she was born, she just seemed a very unhappy baby and cried constantly. I put up with it for six weeks and then my mother suggested an osteopath. He felt that cranial manipulation could relieve the pressure that the forceps had caused. Within two weeks, Emily was a happy, cheerful baby who only cried when she was hungry. I just wish I'd done something sooner.'

Even if your baby is older, cranial osteopathy may help:

'My third child, Joseph, did not cry much in the first months of life. In fact, he was the only one of my children not to receive Infacol for "colic". However, once we started solids at four months, things began to deteriorate, despite taking great care to wean gradually. Between 12 and 18 months of age, he gained no weight and by 18 months he was thoroughly miserable. He cried almost constantly and needed to be carried. He did not play or attempt to talk – he was too miserable. At around 18 months, I took him to a cranial osteopath who diagnosed birth compression in the skull. Over several months of treatment, Joseph improved dramatically. Now, although he is still small, he is a normal two-year-old who plays and talks beautifully.'   *Kerry*

Siobhan, on the other hand, although she didn't take Maeve to see a cranial osteopath until Maeve was three, found that the effects were immediate:

'She had her first treatment and that evening fell asleep on the sofa at 6.30pm. She then slept without a murmur for the next 12 hours. We haven't looked back. We now believe that because of the long labour Maeve had undergone (over 30 hours) she was experiencing some pain or discomfort at the back of her head whenever we laid her down.'

Cranial osteopathy will not help everyone; Naomi, for

example, found that treatment for her son Jacob made only 'a marginal difference'. However, in the course of researching for this book, I heard many success stories from happy parents who believed that the technique (or a related technique called craniosacral therapy, which works on the soft tissues of the neck and skull) had been of great benefit in helping to reduce their baby's crying.

Details of how to find a registered practitioner in your area are given on page 147.

Chiropractic

Chiropractic involves manipulation of the spine to alleviate problems, most often those associated with the neck and the back. The idea is that releasing pressure on the nerves in the spine can have an impact over the whole body. Some chiropractors believe that the technique can be used successfully to treat colic, so this is something you may like to consider if your baby's crying has been given this label.

Reflexology

The thinking behind reflexology, sometimes called zone therapy, is that every part of the body has a corresponding zone in the feet. Gentle massage of the feet at the appropriate point allows the body to 're-balance', clear blocked energy channels and heal itself.

Carrie used reflexology to help her six-month-old daughter Louise, who had been crying persistently for several weeks:

'I felt there was something wrong with one of her ears but I'd taken her to the GP surgery and they hadn't been able to diagnose anything. But Louise couldn't sleep, I felt like I was permanently jet-lagged from the broken nights, and I hated the idea that my daughter was in pain and I was letting her suffer. I was at the end of my tether when someone recommended a reflexologist and I thought it – anything – was worth a try. She pressed quite firmly on Louise's feet for only about two minutes, and on the way home Louise fell into a deep sleep in the pram. The next day there was some redness around the ear but it faded, and Louise never seemed bothered by it again. I'd recommend it to anyone.'

Reflexology is a gentle, non-invasive treatment and if you'd like to find out more about it, there are more details on page 148.

Diet

One of the most common stories I heard from parents when researching for this book was how the adoption of a dairy-free diet had helped to cure a crying baby. In particular, many parents firmly believe that colic is linked to diet, perhaps because all those squirmings and drawing the knees up do look like they're caused by a stomach upset or an adverse reaction to a certain food. The most frequently blamed substance is cow's milk.

While much research has been carried out into this area, the results, unfortunately, are inconclusive and sometimes conflicting. If, one year, a study shows that there is a link between dairy products and crying, then the next year a study will be published which proves the opposite. Nevertheless, despite the scepticism that remains among some health professionals because the link between crying and cow's milk is not as demonstrable or firm as it could be, many parents feel that a change in diet does bring about improvements.

If the baby was breastfed, this meant that the mother had to cut out all dairy produce from her own food intake. If the baby was bottle-fed, this meant switching her to a soya-based alternative, or goat's milk for older babies.

Liz noticed that Florence turned blue around the lips and started squirming shortly after a feed, and it was on the suggestion of her health visitor that she tried a dairy-free diet:

'It took a week or so to make a difference, but Florence definitely became calmer and less agitated. Whether this was because she was nearing the three-month watershed when colic naturally abates anyway, I don't know. But even now, when she's five, Florence reacts badly to milk or cheese, coming out in eczema over her arms, so I'm inclined to think the dairy-free did help and is worth a try.'

Colette, when she was breastfeeding, also decided to exclude all dairy-based products from her own diet:

'It was very difficult to carry out in that I had to watch everything I ate, and this was difficult if we were with family or friends, who always seemed to be offering me milk, cheese, butter, yogurt . . . but in terms of what I would have done to stop the crying, it was easy. If someone had told me that I should stand on my head for ten minutes before every feed, I'd have tried it. I'd have done anything to stop that crying. It took about 24 hours before we noticed a difference, but as I continued with the regime, the colic got less and less and after about two weeks it had gone.'

Check your own nutrition

If you are breastfeeding and think that your baby may be reacting to something in your diet, talk to your health visitor or dietitian. If you decide to go on a dairy-free diet, your health visitor will be able to give you guidance on how to maintain a good calcium intake. This is essential to make sure that the baby's bones develop well and that you yourself do not develop osteoporosis. Never make radical changes to your diet without seeking medical advice.

If you are bottle-feeding and think that your baby may be reacting adversely to cow's milk, ask your health visitor about trying a soya-based or alternative formula milk. This may be available on prescription so talk to your GP as well. Again, such a radical change to a baby's diet must be introduced with caution as some babies can be allergic to soya. Always consult your health visitor first if you are considering making changes to your own diet or your baby's milk.

Sometimes breastfeeding mothers will also say that their baby reacts badly if they have eaten a particular food like eggs or onions. While a true food allergy is almost always accompanied by other symptoms, such as vomiting, fever, rashes or diarrhoea, there is no doubt that the taste of some foods that the mother eats does get into the breast milk and it can be useful to check if a chocolate splurge one day is followed by a crosser-than-usual baby the next.

Rosa thinks that changing to filtered water for making up Harry's bottles rather than tap water helped:

'I was sure all those chemicals in there couldn't be doing him any good, even if they weren't doing him any harm. So I changed to boiled filtered water, or sometimes boiled bottled water. Did it make a difference? I think so.'

If you are thinking of using bottled water, make sure you choose one that does not have a very high mineral content, and always boil it before making up a formula. The mineral content is often stated on the label, but do double-check with your health visitor before using a bottled water.

Food

While current Department of Health Guidelines encourage parents not to give their babies anything other than milk until they are aged at least four months old, and preferably five to six months old, some parents felt that the introduction of solids was the key to less crying:

> 'Marisa was a low birth-weight baby and she had severe colic. Apparently colic is common in low birth-weight babies and they are often poor feeders in the early months. This is something I was told by my paediatrician . . . but not until she was three months old! I definitely felt that solid food helped.' *Majella*

> 'A teaspoon of baby rice every evening just after six o'clock definitely helped. I started this at just after three months and have no regrets. It was that or throttle him.' *Simone*

Visual stimulation

Some babies are not content with the usual baby pursuits like sleeping, feeding and watching the world go by. If they had their way, there would be three-ring circuses laid on every day and firework displays every night. Carla puts much of Hassan's crying down to boredom:

'He was alone in the house with me day after day over a long cold winter. Of course he was bored. I certainly was.'

Amy, too, felt that it helped her to come to terms with the fact that Duncan needed a lot of stimulation:

'When he was about two weeks old I had to accept that he simply wasn't going to sleep, feed and sleep, or sleep as much as all the baby books said he should sleep. So instead of trying to get him to sleep all the time, I concentrated more on entertaining him when he was awake.'

Many parents are unsure in the early days of how to 'play' with their baby, while for others games of mirroring expressions or peek-a-boo come naturally. Experiment all you like, because quite what will entertain your particular baby will vary.

Although other human beings are the best visual stimulation of all, there are other things to try when you can't be there all the time. For some babies a simple mobile, frequently changed, will suffice. Your author, back in the days when babies were put out in the garden in their prams for a good burst of fresh air every morning, no matter what the weather, was apparently entertained for hours on end by the branches of a tree waving above her head. More sophisticated babies like to see balloons bobbing about, tropical aquaria or the neighbour's dog. Amy tried to ring the changes with Duncan:

'I never believed all that stuff about babies' eyes not focusing properly. From the minute he was born Duncan was hungry to see things. He'd gaze intently at the tins in the kitchen cupboard if I showed them to him. I took him out and about as much as I could but because he was so prone to crying bouts, I preferred taking him to outdoor places. There are lots of farms and activity centres in the local area where he could see the lambs being fed or the horses in the field. And if he did start crying, the crying didn't seem so loud outdoors as it did echoing round the local museum.'

There are many places you can take your baby if you're not up to socialising. Once your baby has had his immunisations, you can take him swimming and many pools offer parent-and-child sessions. There may also be a crèche available while you sign up for an aqua-exercise class.

Babies can have their own library cards from birth, and while we're not suggesting that you try first reading skills in between the yells, babies are never too young to look at big, bright picture books. Libraries are much more accommodating of noise than they used to be, and an outing there may give you both a lift.

While sometimes simply getting out of the house and having a change of scene can help, Alex found that she was only able to cope by having a regular rota of activities:

'I concentrated on organising my days. If I made sure I got out every day by going to the baby gym, taking him swimming, going to the mother-and-baby group, having a walk with a friend, then it helped both of us.'

Of course, we don't all have to be as organised as this:

'In the late afternoon, instead of trying to cook or clean, or do anything, I would put Evan in the baby sling and go for a walk through the park and back. And, if we felt like it, through the park and back again.' *Tanya*

If a park does not appeal, why not try what Cathy suggests?

'Find a very noisy street and push the pram up and down it. The baby might still be crying but you won't be able to hear it.'

Cathy also found that an entire change of scene isn't always necessary, as even something small can help:

'If Colin cries I generally change something: a nappy, the way I hold him, turn on some music. It often works.'

Ask for support

Never forget that your GP and health visitor are sources of advice, comfort and reassurance:

'I remember saying to my health visitor how awful I felt at not enjoying being a mother because Lois cried all the time. She said something along the lines of "Every parent of a crying baby feels trapped, miserable, exhausted, angry and frustrated. And now you want to add guilt because you're not enjoying all that?" It really helped because I knew she must see other parents like me, every day, not enjoying it.'

Yvonne

Remember, however, that not everyone will be sympathetic to your plight:

'Ten days after Daisy's birth, my health visitor rolled up. I was crying with exhaustion. "You're not enjoying this phase of your life, are you?" she said. She was a single woman in her late fifties with no children of her own. "Who could enjoy it?" I said. She diagnosed me with postnatal depression and went away again. Weeks later, weeks of sleepless nights, I went to see my GP. He was the father of three teenage children. "The first few weeks are hell," he said. "No one enjoys having a crying baby to deal with night and day." I felt like no one had ever told me this before. This was the first time anyone had admitted that being a parent was different to the image portrayed. It was the reassurance I needed.'   Mary

Helplines like CRY-SIS (for details see page 143) can be a great comfort on the nights when it feels like you're the only one in the world. The CRY-SIS lines are run by parents who have all experienced what it feels like to live with a crying baby. They also know that some of the tried-and-tested 'cures' that are often offered aren't appropriate for every person or every circumstance. They will appreciate, for example, that something as simple as 'establishing a routine' can seem like an impossible task when the parents are suffering from sleep deprivation and the baby is constantly yelling.

'For the first time, when I said how awful it was and how miserable I felt, someone believed me.' *Siobhan*

All calls to helplines are confidential – you don't even have to give your name. This fact alone may give you the confidence to talk more honestly about how you feel. If you feel like your worries are too insignificant, or too dreadful, to share with health professionals who know you, or with friends or relatives who might judge you, then call someone who is willing to listen and is there to answer calls like yours.

The NCT's national special experiences register can put you in touch with other families who have had a colic-affected or constantly crying baby. Talking on a personal level to other parents who are willing to listen, and who can give you support and practical advice on coping, may be just the lifeline you need.

However, sometimes the talking that's required can go beyond a friendly shoulder to cry on:

'The feelings that Harry's crying stirred up in me were very complicated. I felt that although I was trying to love him, I just couldn't engage with him on a very deep level. I couldn't trust myself to give everything to the relationship as I knew I should because when he cried he seemed to be rejecting me so completely. And I felt guilty all the time that I didn't love him. I kept thinking more and more about my own childhood and, after talking with my partner, decided that this was the thing I really needed to understand. I had several months of sessions with a psychotherapist to explore these feelings. Looking back on the past and getting it all into focus wasn't easy, but it helped me to understand why I was reacting the way I was. Once I knew this, I was able to begin shedding old fears and respond to Harry as an individual, as a person in his own right. It's still a challenge some days, but at least I now know why I was cutting myself off from him.'

Rosa

Socialising

I've left this one until last because, while it will never 'cure' a crying baby, it can alleviate all the other symptoms that a crying baby can cause – loss of confidence, lack of self-esteem and a sense of being trapped – so profoundly that, while the problem doesn't go away, it helps parents to see it in a whole new light. This was the case for Amy:

'We'd moved shortly before Duncan was born so I knew no one in the local area, and I missed work dreadfully. In the first week or so, there were lots of phone calls and visits from relatives and friends but these gradually tailed off and the only other adult who I could be guaranteed to talk to once a week was the health visitor. Duncan cried so much and was so demanding that I could see the months ahead stretching before me like a prison sentence. It was only as I made new friends that the bars of the cage were opened.'

'I found life was far more bearable when I was not at home. Natalie was distracted and cried far less, and I had some companionship, particularly at NCT coffees. It was a way I could get some intellectual stimulation and interest in my life, and somewhere I could take my very-reliant-on-the-breast baby.'   *Cathy*

Don't feel that in the early days, when you thank your lucky stars if you've managed to get dressed by midday, you are obliged to embark on a whirlwind round of social engagements. It can take courage and determination to get yourself there, and walking into a room of strangers is never easy for most of us, even at the best of times. When you've got rings under your eyes, milk spattered on your shoulder and a baby who is yelling solidly, it can be daunting.

'I expected everyone to look like a picture from a magazine, and to have these sweet little babies who sat in their baskets and cooed all the time. It was quite a revelation that some people looked tireder than me and their babies could yell even more loudly.'   *Amy*

Amy was gradually eased into a wider circle of friends by making use of a local NCT member she had met at the clinic, who went with her to the first few social events. Alex was also fearful at first about going somewhere new, but found that it was worth the risk:

'Finally, when he was about six months old, I plucked up courage to take Joshua along to a mother-and-baby group. He watched the other babies and played with the toys and was as good as gold. Best of all, I met other mothers with similarly aged babies and we chatted about everything – sleep, pelvic floors, nappy rash, loneliness, missing work. Everyone was really friendly and understanding. When I got home, my partner couldn't believe the difference in me. For the first time in months, I was smiling.'

Outings can have their worries at first:

'I used to hate it when Bethany cried when we were out. I used to think she was alerting the world to the fact that I was an inadequate mother, that I didn't know what to do.'   *Helen*

There's no guarantee that you won't bump into the odd parent who's finding life with a new baby a breeze, and who stares hard at you every time yours cries, but thankfully such experiences are rare (and she'll understand one day when *she* has one who cries). Most mothers find mother-and-baby groups or social events an invaluable source of support. This was the case for Nicole:

> 'I managed to keep my sanity by turning up at the majority of baby groups going. It was the support I found there that got me through it all. To be able to tell someone that my life had turned into a nightmare and hear them agree how awful coping with a crying baby could be . . . this was what I needed to hear.'

If your baby cries incessantly, it means that your confidence has already taken a hard knock. The prospect of socialising may seem to demand more confidence than you've got left, especially when you're already depressed and under stress from your crying baby. Of all things to do with your crying baby, however, this one can be the most valuable . . . and not just for yourself, either.

> 'It took a while but I gradually made some really close friends in those first few months. One night I got a call from one of them and her baby had been awake since lunchtime, refusing to feed, crying . . . all the things I knew so well. It made me realise she needed me as a friend just as much as I needed her.'
>
> *Amy*

Health visitors usually run clinics where they can check your baby's growth and development, and often there is tea, coffee and a chance to talk to other mothers, too. These can be a useful starting point for meeting other parents. Also, keep an eye on the noticeboards in health centres, libraries and supermarkets – these can give you information about other activities on offer in your area, and details of any local contacts for the NCT and other organisations.

Many NCT branches run postnatal exercise classes and discussion groups and these can be a very good way to meet other parents in the area who have a baby of a similar age to your own. Look in the phone book under NCT for the name of your local contact, who will be able to give you more information, or call 0181 992 8637 for details of your local branch. Remember, you do not have to be an NCT member to take part in activities and social events.

Accepting

It may be some time before you find something that works for you and your baby, but Michele feels it is important to keep trying:

'Even if you are angry and exhausted, it is worth doing all you can to help your crying baby. I think the baby will know that you are trying to comfort him.'

Of course, for some babies there will be no miracle cure. Something will soothe them one day but not the next. This was what Carla found with Hassan:

'Hassan cried a great deal from the age of one or two days until he reached about 18 months. Some screaming fits would last for two hours. He'd want to be cuddled then he'd throw himself on the floor, writhe about, fling himself on the sofa, roll off . . . it was all I could do to stop him hitting his head. As far as I could see, nothing brought on these attacks. He'd be peaceful one minute and screaming the next. We never found out what caused it. At first we put it down to insecurity, then hunger, then of course everyone said it was colic and I tried every possible remedy for that, but nothing worked. Then we thought it might be teething: more remedies, no success. Eventually I decided it was just the way he was. It didn't suddenly stop, but it just faded out and he gradually became a more peaceful child. Now he's three and he's well-balanced, friendly and mixes well. I thought it was going to go on for ever but it did pass.'

Carla ends her letter with the line: 'We survived.' Sometimes simply surviving feels like a punishment but, as Carla's experience shows, even the longest phase of crying will pass eventually.

Some parents find that simply trying one more piece of advice after another is demoralising because nothing seems to work and they feel even more of a failure. If you feel this way, or if you feel that you've tried enough strategies and don't want to push yourself over the edge by trying any more, being accepting of yourself and your baby may bring some comfort, as it did for Alex:

> 'Joshua is still "one of those babies" and nothing can be done to change that. The only thing I could change was the way I reacted to him. To get through, I had to accept the fact that this is how he was and stop focusing on the negative aspects of his behaviour. It's worth trying everything you can if you are unlucky enough to get a baby like this, even though, like me, you may never know why he cries so persistently. It is hard, but if you can't change your baby, you can change the way you react towards him.'

> 'In the end we had to conclude that George was one of those babies who didn't like being a baby. Once we knew that a large part of his crying came from his frustration and lack of control, we weren't able to stop the crying but we were able to deal with it much better because it didn't seem directed personally against us.'   *Maria*

Both Maria and Alex are parents who found that nothing 'worked', there was no miracle cure, but the key to being able to cope was to focus on the positive, which will become clearer with each passing day.

5

Special situations

Colic

Doctors are divided on whether 'colic' exists. However, if you have a baby under six months old who screams uncontrollably every evening, then you might as well call it colic, because you still have to deal with it, whatever it's called. The label itself won't make a bit of difference. And the label won't hide the fact that caring for a baby with 'colic' is one of the most relentless, frustrating and confidence-shattering experiences a new parent can face.

'Colic' is a term used to describe a particular pattern of crying. Babies seem to suffer inconsolable misery and apparent pain, often drawing their knees up towards their stomachs, clenching their fists and screwing up their faces. Many parents speak of the 'colic cry', a high-pitched scream, urgent and full of distress.

The distinctive bouts of crying usually start around three to four weeks of age and peak at about six to eight weeks. Babies with colic cry for several hours at a stretch, often in the evenings. Sometimes the baby can be soothed for a short while, but the crying soon starts again, for no discernible reason. In every other respect, babies with colic are usually happy, healthy and developing normally.

Colic rarely lasts more than three months, although some babies show symptoms until they are around five months old.

Babies in developed countries are much more prone to colic than babies in non-industrialised countries, although the reasons for this are not yet fully understood.

Is it something serious?

If your new-born is crying for prolonged periods, and you can't see any reason for it, it is best to get your baby checked by a GP first, before putting the crying down to 'colic'. There may be some physical problem causing the crying, and it's essential to rule out the possibility of something more serious.

But if colic is nothing more than a particular pattern of crying, what causes it? The medical profession still isn't sure, despite decades of study; there are no definitive answers, but many interesting theories.

Because classic 'colic' is often accompanied by the baby drawing up his legs, or squirming as if afflicted by wind, many parents and some doctors believe that it is caused by an intestinal disturbance or an immaturity of the new-born's nervous system. One view is that colic is caused by fluid from the stomach regurgitating back into the oesophagus (a process known as reflux), which happens because the valve at the top of the baby's stomach is still immature. Because of this view, parents whose babies have colic are often advised to keep them as upright as possible during feeding.

Others see trapped air as the cause – although this may be air swallowed because of the crying, rather than air there in the first place.

Other experts dismiss ideas that colic is due to wind or digestive disturbance and see burping as a wasted effort. They point out that the stomachs of colicky babies often feel hard simply because the baby is using these muscles to cry.

Colic seems to occur often in 'high-needs' babies who have sensitive temperaments. It seems to affect somewhere between 10% and 20% of babies, but this statistic alone cannot convey the emotionally devastating effects on a family with a colicky baby. Many parents, especially if this is their first child, are convinced that it is caused by some-thing they are, or are not, doing:

'I used to think, "It's all my fault. It's because I don't know what to do or I'm not doing it right." That feeling was very hard to shake off.'   *Liz*

Jane, too, had similar feelings, even though Esther was her fifth baby:

'She seemed to be in so much pain, and only slept, if I held her, for about ten minutes. I felt inadequate and frustrated, especially because with this baby I could hardly be called an "anxious novice"! This was one reason for the crying I'd been told in the past.'

Many parents whose babies were affected by colic said that it was reassuring to know that there was nothing physically wrong with their baby, but that didn't make it any easier to deal with:

'I used to watch Harry kick and scream and draw his legs up, look at his red face, his clenched fists, and I felt so helpless because I was certain that this baby was suffering and there was nothing I could do about it.'   *Rosa*

Maria also found the experience shattering:

'Colic. It's such a little word but do doctors have any idea what it means? Just as Peter came in through the door in the evening, when he was tired and I was desperate for adult conversation, the four or five hours of screaming would start and with it a horrible, sick feeling in my stomach. George screamed until his face was plastered with sweat, deathly pale, with his lips blue. Peter and I would look at one another and hate our helplessness, and sometimes each other for not being able to stop this.'

The colic crisis

The saddest thing about colic is that, whatever causes it, very little seems to help. There are some strategies that other parents have found helpful and you may find it helpful, too, to have some definite techniques to try, rather than spend the evening 'crying time' simply feeling helpless:

❏ Try giving your baby a cuddle and a warm bath
❏ Swaddle him firmly so that he feels secure
❏ Lie him on a well-wrapped, warm hot-water bottle on your lap
❏ Try using colic drops or gripe water
❏ Some babies respond well to a massage
❏ If it soothes your baby, let him suck a dummy, perhaps with the aim of weaning him gently off it again when the colic crisis is over
❏ Alternative therapies may also offer some comfort, particularly if they help to relax you and your baby.

The sugar solution

Recently, some doctors have been suggesting small doses of sugar-water as a soothing mechanism for babies with colic. One study (carried out at the Department of Paediatrics, University of Bergen, Norway) found that 12 out of 19 colic-affected babies who were given a sugar solution improved, with five of them stopping crying immediately. It may be that the taste of sugar produces endorphins, natural 'happiness' hormones within the body, and that's the key factor. There's also no need to worry about your child's teeth because as babies have colic at a very young age, it is unlikely that they will have come through yet.

If you'd like to give this a try with your baby:

❑ Dissolve three teaspoons of sugar in a cup of boiling water and leave this to cool.
❑ Use a small syringe or a teaspoon to dribble about 2ml of the solution into your baby's mouth; dribbling it into the side of the mouth will help your baby to swallow it more easily.

You can keep the solution in the refrigerator for up to 24 hours.

If there is no improvement within an hour, try one of the other remedies as it seems that further doses of the sugar solution will have little effect.

The colic barrier

Colic seems to be a self-limiting condition in that babies simply do grow out of it. The most common age seems to be around three months – the colic barrier – although it may persist a little longer. While this may be some comfort, it may also mean that people don't always take you seriously and will cheerfully tell you 'She'll grow out of it,' as if this was all the solution you needed.

'I felt so helpless and angry at the "oh, they grow out of it" approach. Thomas was crying for a reason and I couldn't help him. He had classic "evening" colic but would also yell for two or three hours in the mid-morning. And this went on following the three-month "finale" that doctors suggest you wait for.'   *Jane*

Nevertheless, knowing that it will pass may help you to accept it as a phase, one that you can actively cope with, rather than blaming yourself or fruitlessly looking for 'causes'. Or perhaps you could stop looking for remedies, too, as Majella suggests:

'I tried everything suggested for colic and, quite frankly, nothing worked. There is no cure for colicky babies. If there was one, we'd all know about it. They do grow out of it and in Marisa's case it took four months. Four months is a long time. I found that being able to tell someone how I felt, and having some company around me, did me much more good in the end than pinning my hopes on colic drops.'

One final word of comfort. Colic will cause no lasting harm to the baby. And while you may look back on those dark evenings with despair, your baby won't remember it at all.

Teething

First teeth usually appear around four to six months but, if the trials and tribulations of parents are anything to go by, they often make their presence felt long before that. Yvonne felt that Lois was 'born teething'. Julie, too, felt that teething started early and caused far more pain than she'd expected.

> 'If I could change one thing about my daughter's first year of life, it would be to make sure Amy was born with her teeth already through. She was miserable and upset for weeks before each one appeared at the surface of the gum, and when they started to cut through, she was inconsolable. And no sooner was one through than the next one would start. Teething made my life a misery.'

If your baby dribbles a lot, has swollen gums, and cries as if in pain, then I think it's safe to say that she might be bothered by teeth coming through, no matter how old she is. Some of the strategies that other parents have tried are listed in the box opposite.

Teething tips

❏ Offer a peeled raw carrot straight from the fridge.

❏ Protect the skin around his mouth from the dribble by smoothing on a thin film of petroleum jelly.

❏ Try rubbing gums gently with a teething gel (and a clean finger). Your pharmacist can recommend one without sugar so that emerging teeth aren't put at risk of decay.

❏ Give a little infant paracetamol (following the directions on the box) to relieve pain.

❏ If your baby also has diarrhoea, a rash or a fever, don't just put these down to 'teething'; ask your GP to check that everything's OK.

Some children seem to react exceptionally badly to teething and, for a few of these, very little seems to help.

> 'I tried teething gels, homoeopathic granules, teething rings, carrots . . . none of it made an impression, and baby paracetamol just made her drowsy but still miserable.'
> *Julie*

Julie, however, finally found that acupuncture helped both her and Amy. Acupuncture is an ancient Chinese system which involves placing specially designed needles into the body at specific points to focus and channel the body's natural energies. Although Julie was initially sceptical, she found the treatment worked:

'At around 14 months, Amy started cutting her first molars, and things went from bad to worse. She started refusing all food and was waking up feverish in the night. In the end, I met a woman whose son had been treated with acupuncture and I made an appointment. I was a bit sceptical, but was assured that acupuncture could help and that many children had been treated successfully before. I was also told that a few babies do react badly to teething and consequently heat builds up in their bodies. Putting the needles in at certain points helps to dissipate the heat and helps them to cope better. The needles didn't make Amy even wince, and they were only in for a few seconds. The treatment made her drowsy and she slept brilliantly that night, and also started eating again. We never looked back. Amy had several more treatments over the next few months and by the time it came to her last molars, she cut them without a murmur.'

If your child is crying and unhappy with teething, perhaps acupuncture or other complementary therapies are worth considering. This is one area where orthodox medicine seems to be able to offer very little comfort or relief. Always consult a registered acupuncturist. Details of how to find one in your area are given on page 145.

Eczema

Children who suffer from this distressing condition are often quite genuinely (and understandably) miserable and so will often cry a lot. Parents whose child wakes to scratch will often be more reluctant to adopt techniques such as controlled crying because they feel that their child is under such stress already, they don't want to add to it. Karin, who found that controlled crying worked well for her first baby, Megan, could not adopt the same approach with Myriam:

> 'She used to scratch so much, through the gloves and everything, that she bled. I knew there was no way I could leave her to cry, even for five minutes. Instead, from very early on, I instituted a strict bedtime routine: bath, cream, milk, bed, with it all taking only half an hour. Perhaps because she sensed my firmness right from the start, she didn't wake nearly as often as Megan had.'

With eczema, as with all special situations, it is easy to add guilt to your whirlwind of emotions, and easy to be hard on yourself. If you can allow yourself time to meet your own needs as well as the baby's, the whole family will benefit.

Twins or more

If the sound of one crying baby is agony, some parents of twins, triplets or more go through sheer torture. For them, many of the problems of tiredness and exhaustion are doubled (or tripled) as they struggle just to keep up with the feeding, changing, housework and washing. In many cases one parent, usually the father, will work longer hours to cover the additional costs that multiples incur, so isolation and loneliness can become real problems. One trick that parents of twins learn perhaps quicker than most is to accept all offers of help. If you aren't offered help, ask for it.

> 'There were days in the early weeks when I didn't know which way was up. The boys never woke in the night at the same time, and they could wake up to eight times each, they never wanted to feed at the same time . . . the days were just a blur. Eventually Tom came home late one evening and found me in tears and both babies screaming. He said "What can I do?" I said, "You can take a week off work." If he hadn't, I think I'd have left them on the hospital doorstep.'
>
> *Jo*

Isa is another parent of twins who only coped in the early weeks because she had extra support:

> 'When Rob went back to work, his parents came to stay for a week and to be honest I was dreading it as

we'd never been close before and I was sure they would blame me if one of the girls cried, as they did fairly often. But they helped in so many practical ways, not just with the shopping and the washing, but by taking Annie out for an hour while I fed and bathed Lily, or by simply walking up and down the hall with Lily while I comforted Annie.'

Extra emotional and practical support is especially valuable for establishing breastfeeding:

'I couldn't get the hang of feeding first at all. Was it one on the right side, one on the left? Together? Separately? And they both wanted to latch on in different positions. We spent a lot of the early days crying, all three of us, until a midwife at the hospital, who'd been away on holiday, came back and sorted us out.'   *Jeanne*

Parents of twins come under perhaps the most pressure to bottle-feed or to introduce solids at a young age at the slightest hint of a crying baby, even though the laws of supply and demand still work and, if you have two babies, you will produce enough milk for two babies. Parents of triplets or more usually accept that some complementary feeding will be necessary and working out rotas of feeding, changing and comforting can be hard work even when two parents can be there all the time. Enlist every source of support that you can.

Extra support for parents of twins or more

❏ Ask relatives to come to stay and make it clear that they are being asked to help.

❏ See if your local social services department will provide you with a home help.

❏ If you can afford one, an au pair or mother's help will be invaluable, and may mean that you and your partner can get out together one evening a week.

❏ Offer yourself as a 'parent placement' to your local nursery nurse training college. Students often make a special study of twins and will be able to help out for several weeks, or for one day a week.

❏ Keep in close touch with your health visitor and ask her to support you as much as you need; for example, by coming to you to weigh the babies, rather than having to take them to the clinic.

❏ Get in touch with the nearest Twins Club. They will know all about extra resources and places you can go with your twins in the local area.

Establishing a good sleep pattern is vital for parents of twins if they are not to lapse into exhaustion, although with twins this can sometimes be harder. While some babies will sleep soundly through the wails of their sibling, others will stir at the least murmur. In such cases parents often rush to attend to them so that one crying doesn't 'set the other off'.

For Jeanne, working to a checklist of 'needs' helped:

> 'I would mentally go through the list. Are they hungry? Do they need a clean nappy? Are they hot? Do they want their dummy? And if all else failed, then I would leave one to cry it out while I went through the list with the other. Sometimes I left them to cry it out at opposite ends of the house while I took ten minutes to load the washing machine and do the dishes.'

Getting out of the house is often more problematic for parents of twins. Isa, for example, found that a twin pram that someone lent to her was far too heavy for her to be able to push, so she solved the problem of being able to get out and relieve the tension in another way:

> 'We bought one single buggy and a sling and the girls took turns in one or the other. I could carry one while pushing the other in the pram. It meant that going out was more manageable and I think both of them benefited from the extra physical contact. It meant I knew I could go out as well, so the feeling of being trapped with the crying all day did lessen.'

If you can use your resourcefulness and your ingenuity to find ways to relieve the burden of isolation when you have twins and at least one of them cries, you will have taken a major step forward in solving the crying 'problem'. Although socialising can seem like one more thing you don't have time for, if you can give yourself permission to take time to meet other parents, you will find that the benefits outweigh the difficulties, because meeting other parents of twins can be one of the greatest sources of support you will ever have.

Premature babies

If parents have difficulty adjusting to the arrival of a baby who turns up round about the expected date, how much more adjustment do parents of premature babies have to make? The baby may look very different to the full-term, chubby infant of their dreams and is sometimes out of parents' reach behind perspex, kept alive by complex equipment. In some cases parents have to wait for weeks or months to discover if their child will have a disability, or will live. Many parents keep themselves safe by distancing themselves from the baby. Others feel so emotionally linked to their baby that the rest of life seems to stop. This was the case for Paula:

'I think I sort of held myself back from her while she was in the SCBU, but when they said she would soon be able to come home, I started spending more time with her. We'd been looking forward to bringing her home, I couldn't wait. And it was wonderful the first couple of days, to be able to look after her.

But then the crying started and what we'd been looking forward to for so long became a catastrophe.'

Parents of premature babies are often overwhelmed by their baby's fragile body and some feel hesitant about cuddling or comforting them when they cry:

'Harriet's arms and legs were like little sticks. I wanted to pick her up but was frightened of crushing her.'   *Richard*

Premature babies or babies who are small for their birth date often have more piercing or distressing cries than term babies, and often more feeding difficulties and bouts of colic. Because their stomachs are correspondingly smaller, premature babies may need to feed more often and their cries of hunger will reflect this.

The way that parents react to their premature babies when they cry can often be different, too. Beth had this experience with Lisette, her second child:

'Lisette was born by caesarean more than a month early and she was in quite severe pain from the awkward position she had jammed herself into against my pelvis. The skin on her back was raw and abscessed, and it was very difficult to find a position for breastfeeding where we could both be comfortable, so the early days involved a lot of crying on both sides as I tried to get her to latch on. And I couldn't bear it. I couldn't bear to hear her cry. I felt that she'd been through so much pain already

I didn't want to inflict any more distress on her. When we got home it was even worse. At her first murmur I jumped, the way I never had with Stephan.'

Coral, too, found that she was super-sensitive to her son Anthony's cries:

'He was so tiny, his voice was so tiny. He was just so pathetic. I felt his crying was like an accusation that the world had already started treating him badly and I wanted to make up for that. I think I carried him around constantly for almost the first two months after he came out of the SCBU because he never seemed to settle. I didn't even want my partner to hold him. Only I would do. Needless to say, I was crippled by tiredness, but so guilty I didn't know how to change things. It was only as we reached the time when he would have been out in the world anyway than I stopped being so highly strung and started treating his crying like that of a normal baby. I was suddenly able to say, "What am I going to do about this situation?" instead of feeling I just had to live with it.'

Many pre-term or low birth-weight babies respond best to low-key methods of soothing – swaddling, lullabies, patting and contact. Over-stimulating them with too much entertainment can sometimes be too much:

'What Holly liked was everything calm, quiet and peaceful. I found a dummy was a lifesaver in those early days as she seemed to want to get wrapped up in herself, and she gradually emerged from this self-absorption at around five months old.'   *Clare*

While most babies leave the crying phase behind them when they are three months old, with premature babies it can persist longer, usually up to around five months, so be prepared for this.

Babies with disabilities

Discovering that your new-born has any problem, whether it's a dislocated hip, a more severe and long-term disability or an illness that may need prolonged treatment, is traumatic. If, on top of this, your baby is in pain or made miserable by the effect of the disability, you will feel helpless, heartbroken and distraught. You need help and support. There are many organisations that can offer specialised advice and support, and your doctor or health visitor will be able to give your information about these. No one I have ever spoken to has found that they didn't get some benefit from talking to someone else whose child had a similar disability.

Even as a baby, the child with a disability is usually much harder for the parents to look after. She may be a difficult feeder, or just very slow. She may have fits, or require constant medication, or there may be plasters and splints to deal with. In addition, there will be visits to therapists, specialists and consultants to fit in alongside all the usual demands of a new baby. Her care and development will need a great deal of concentration on behalf of the parents.

A child who is born with a disability will sometimes cry far more – and sometimes cry far less – than other babies, but parents whose disabled baby cries are often reluctant to make use of some of the mechanisms for coping which allow themselves time off. They may be apprehensive about letting someone else look after the baby, taking some time together as a couple, or leaving the baby alone. Monica's baby, Lindsay has Down's syndrome:

'Whenever she cried, I felt guilty. She was already at such a disadvantage in the world that I hated to see her upset. Now I realise I got myself into the position of being a martyr to it all and whenever she cried felt I had to go to her immediately, and it had to be me, no one else would do. When she was around six months old, I saw my GP, who prescribed anti-depressants, because by then I was low all the time and could hardly face another day. I think they helped, but what helped more was letting my partner take over more. I hadn't realised it, but my behaviour was making him feel excluded.'

Many of the ways discussed in this book will help parents whose child has a disability, although these parents often need support and encouragement to try them in the first place. Your health visitor is a good source of advice and information, and always talk to her, or to one of the helplines, if you are finding it difficult to cope.

6

As your baby grows . . .

Putting it all in perspective

As babies grow, their crying becomes more communica-
tive, particular patterns develop, and you can feel more
confident about adapting your responses to your baby's
needs. This is something that Sandra discovered:

'I used to go to Callum the first time he cried at
night, every time, although I became totally
exhausted in the process. Eventually one night I just
left him, hoping he would go back to sleep, and he
did! Now I've worked out that the first time he
wakes, he'll just give a gentle murmur and a snuffle,
as if he's turning over in his sleep, and then he'll
drop off again for another three-quarters of an hour
or so. When he wakes again, this time it's for real
and he really does need a feed.'

One of the key things to remember is that research shows that babies who cry show no long-term effects. Several of the parents who wrote to me while I was researching for this book sent me photographs of their families, and in every case I was struck by how beautiful and well adjusted and happy the children who had been 'crying babies' had grown to be. You couldn't tell from looking at them which ones had been such a problem in the past. Holding on to the fact that there is nothing physically wrong with your baby and that she *will* just 'grow out of it' may help.

While you're in the thick of it, that may feel like small comfort. But perhaps another idea to hold on to is the fact that there is some anecdotal evidence to suggest that, in the long term, some parents feel more attached to a baby who tested them with excessive crying. It seems as if the hours of extra care and worry do not damage the bond between parent and child but can even make it stronger.

Marianne feels that something of this is true:

'Caroline required a lot of work when she was tiny. Although I hated every minute of it at the time, and often felt quite distant from her, now I feel I know her really well.'

Amy also feels that the hours she spent in close contact with Duncan have brought them a deeper relationship:

'I feel I understand Duncan much more than his sister, who was a sunny, cheerful soul from the start.

All those hours I walked the bedroom floor at nights, singing to him and rocking him. It made a bond between us that can never be broken.'

Carla feels that Hassan's troubled babyhood did not cause him long-term problems:

'He's three now and we haven't had any major problems with toddler tantrums, not anything near the trouble some of my friends have had. Perhaps he got all the frustration out of his system early. He still wakes sometimes in the night, but he is quite happy to go downstairs, get a snack or drink from the fridge, play with his toys and then go back to sleep!'

Kate, however, feels that the stresses of the crying phase have left their mark:

'It would be nice to report that Alice is now a happy, secure seven-year-old but she is still afraid of being alone so always brings whatever she is doing to the same room as we are in. Our relationship, although close, is often fiery, due, I suspect, to the strain of her first few years.'

Veronica, too, feels that there have been repercussions:

'As Rochelle grew, I felt I was constantly struggling with our relationship. I'm always trying not to be short with her and I know this started in the early days. It upsets me now to feel what I missed.'

Several other parents mentioned that the babies in the family who had been the most prone to crying and sleep problems were also more likely to suffer from nightmares as they grew. They also often had a greater need for 'cuddlies' and security blankets:

> 'Scott, Rachel and Angus are all avid thumb-suckers, and have cuddlies, while my other two don't.' *Debra*

Yet Debra also found that her babies who cried were also the ones who talked earlier and walked earlier.

Talking it through

Some parents find that it is years later that they want to talk to someone about the emotional toll that the 'crying years' have taken. Amy didn't tell anyone how she really felt until her first child, Duncan, was nearly ten:

> 'It all came out in a rush. Not to a therapist, not to a health professional, not even to my husband. I was just talking one night to a friend about when our children were tiny and suddenly I started talking about how trapped and limited I felt when alone in the house with Duncan day after day. I loved him so much but felt so angry that I'd had to cope with this constant crying all alone. It just wasn't how I'd pictured things. All the pent-up anger surprised even me.'

Kate feels the need to talk but doesn't feel she has the right opportunity:

> 'It would be brilliant to talk through all our concerns with someone but I don't want to be labelled "a problem" as might happen if we attended family therapy.'

Another crying baby?

For some parents, the effects of having to cope with a crying baby are so profound, and they are brought so low by the experience, that they are reluctant to contemplate having another child. Some parents wrote of having 'plucked up courage' to have a second, or third. Cathy says that it was 'Never again!' until Natalie was about three years old and she felt confident enough to try for a second.

> 'There's a seven-year gap between ours, and I think this was because by then my selective memory had shut a lot out.'
> *Naomi*

Others, like Michele, decide that they cannot risk it:

> 'Looking back, I don't know how I coped with Georgia and her almost constant crying. I certainly wouldn't contemplate having another child.'

However, sometimes parents whose first baby cried find that things are easier second time around:

> 'Stuart started off well, feeding and sleeping better than Alice ever did. I also found it easier to inter-pret his different cries. Whether this was down to me or because he gave clearer signals, I don't know.'
>
> *Kate*

Liz, on the other hand, found that while her first baby, Luke, had been a 'dream baby', very content and easy to handle, her second, Florence, was a complete surprise:

> 'She cried incessantly, night, day, it made no differ-ence. Luckily because I'd had such an easy time of it with Luke, I knew it couldn't be something I was doing that was wrong. The problem had to be external – which is why I went on a dairy-free diet – or internal to her; she was simply naturally prone to colic.'

Sue says that she is contemplating a second child and feels that, even if the next baby does turn out to cry as much as Simon did, this time she will be better able to cope:

> 'If you'd asked me when Simon was, say, three months old, I'd have told you that there was no way I was ever going to have another baby. But this time I'm prepared: I've made a lot of friends locally, and I didn't have that with Simon. I also don't have the unrealistic expectations of falling in love with a

baby like a bolt from the blue – although it might happen. I know that tiny babies gradually become more sociable, more interesting, because I've seen Simon grow. But perhaps more than anything, having had the experience of Simon, I know that however soul-destroying the crying can be, I can come out the other side.'

Siobhan is glad she had a second child:

'Roisin restored our confidence in our abilities as parents. More than anything, it made us believe we were not to blame for Maeve's unhappiness.'

Don't blame yourself

Whatever your situation, whether this is your first, third or fifth baby, whether she cries all day or cries all night, perhaps the most important thing to remember is that you are not alone and you are not to blame. Mary now says, looking back:

'I am amazed now how naive I was trying to stop the crying all the time. Babies do cry. It isn't because you've done anything wrong, they just do. I wish someone had told me that sooner.'

When things are at their blackest, it may help to remind yourself that other people have been there and understand even the darkest of feelings. Looking back on her early days with Georgia, Michele now says:

> 'The one thing I didn't do was accept help. I wish I had. I just felt I was being very poor in the role of mother and had to get better. This wasn't the case. I was actually doing very well.'

Like Michele, you are probably doing very well, too, and if you can recognise this fact and accept that the crying is not your fault, then it may be the breakthrough you need.

Resources

The organisations listed here can provide you with a wide variety of information, advice and support. This is not an exhaustive list. There are many other charities and organisations which can offer support for a rare disorder or specific syndrome that may be at the heart of your child's distress. Your GP or health visitor will be able to give you more details of these. If you are writing to any of the organisations listed here, don't forget to include a stamped addressed envelope as many of these organisations are small and rely on fund-raising and donations to survive.

Also, don't forget that your health visitor or social services department will be able to give you information about support groups and networks in your area. Your local library and GP practice noticeboards are also good ways of finding out what groups meet near you.

Inevitably, telephone numbers change. We have made every effort to make sure that the information given here is as up to date as it possibly can be. If you become aware of any changes, we would love to hear from you so that we can put these details right in our next edition.

Breastfeeding

National Childbirth Trust (NCT)
If you contact your local branch, they will be able to put you in touch with a trained breastfeeding counsellor who lives nearby. The support and guidance of a breastfeeding counsellor is available to all and you do not have to be an NCT member to use this service, for which there is no charge. All counsellors are mothers who have breastfed their own children. If you are having difficulties with breastfeeding or lack confidence with feeding your baby, you may find talking to a breastfeeding counsellor helpful. If you need details of your local branch, contact NCT headquarters at:
Alexandra House
Oldham Terrace
London W3 6NH
Tel: 0181 992 8637

Association of Breastfeeding Mothers
Gives support and information to breastfeeding mothers.
PO Box 207
Bridgwater TA6 7YT
Tel: 0171 813 1481

The Breastfeeding Network
Write for more information about their breastfeeding
counsellors if you feel that your baby's crying is connected
with feeding difficulties.
PO Box 11126
Paisley PA2 8YB

La Leche League
Breastfeeding mothers will find that this organisation can
provide a wealth of information and ideas. There are local
groups in many areas of the country where you can meet
other breastfeeding mothers for mutual support.
BM 3424
London WC1N 3XX
Tel: 0171 242 1278

Helplines

All helplines listed here are confidential. Your call will
usually be answered by someone who has experience of
your situation and knows how you feel. They are a unique
opportunity to share your problems and combat stress.

Serene
Serene incorporates the CRY-SIS helpline and support
group for parents of babies who have sleep problems and/
or who cry excessively. The helpline is open 24 hours a
day, seven days a week for emotional support and practical

advice. Between the hours of 8am to 11pm, they will be able to put you in touch with a trained counsellor.
Telephone: 0171 404 5011

Infacol Colic Helpline
Open 5pm–10pm Monday to Friday. Provides advice about colic for parents from a trained nurse.
Tel: 0181 994 9874

Parentline
This national helpline offers advice and support to all parents under stress.
Tel: 01702 559900

TAMBA Twinline
This listening and information service is open Monday to Friday 7pm–11pm; Saturday and Sunday 10am–11pm. The call will be answered by someone who is a parent of twins or more themselves and they can give you up-to-date information on a wide range of issues and support in stressful situations.
Tel: 01732 868000

Complementary therapies

If you are undecided about which therapy may be best for you and your baby, you can find out more about complementary therapies by sending two first–class stamps to:

The Complementary Medical Association
The Meridian, 142a Greenwich High Road
London SE10 8NN

Many complementary therapists can be found in the *Yellow Pages* (often under 'Clinics') but try asking around first for a personal recommendation. Each therapy has its own organisation and register and you can make sure that the person you choose to treat you is appropriately qualified by checking with the relevant organisation or with:

The British Register of Complementary Practitioners
PO Box 194
London SE16 1QZ
Tel: 0171 237 5165
Fax: 0171 237 5175

Complementary therapies are rarely available within the NHS, although some health centres do have an attached osteopath, for example, and can refer you on. It may be worth asking your GP about this. Charges for services are usually very reasonable and a good therapist will always explain clearly the costs involved. Some clinics that treat children do so on a sliding scale so that no one is unable to benefit from treatment because of a low income.

Acupuncture

The British Acupuncture Council
Park House, 206–208 Latimer Road
London W10 6RE
Tel: 0181 964 0222

Aromatherapy

International Federation of Aromatherapists
2–4 Chiswick High Road
London W14 1TH
Tel: 0181 742 2605

Chiropractic

British Chiropractic Association
Can help you find a registered practitioner in your area.
Tel: 0118 950 5950

Herbal remedies

National Institute of Medical Herbalists
56 Longbrook Street
Exeter EX4 6AH
Tel: 01392 426022

Homoeopathy

The British Homoeopathic Association
Send a 60p SAE (A4) for a list of homoeopathic doctors.
27a Devonshire Street
London W1N 1RJ
Tel: 0171 935 2163

The Society of Homoeopaths
For more information about homoeopathy, send an SAE.
The Society can help you find a registered homoeopath in
your area.
2 Artizan Road
Northampton NN1 4HU
Tel: 01604 621400

Massage

**International Association of Infant Massage (UK
Branch)**
Can help you find a registered practitioner in your area
who is experienced in working with babies.
Tel: 0115 903 9595

Osteopathy

Osteopathic Centre for Children
109 Harley Street
London W1N 1DG
Tel: 0171 486 6160

Osteopathic Information Service
For further information about osteopathy, send an SAE.
The Osteopathic Information Service can also help you find
a registered practitioner of cranial osteopathy in your area.
PO Box 2074
Reading
Berkshire RG1 4YR
Tel: 0118 512051

You may also like to contact The General Council and Register of Osteopaths for names of fully qualified practitioners.
Tel: 01734 576585

Reflexology

Holistic Association of Reflexologists
92 Sheering Road
Old Harlow
Essex CM17 0JW
Tel: 01279 429060
Fax: 01279 445234

Counselling

British Association for Counselling
The Association can provide you with details of qualified counsellors working in your area.
1 Regent Place
Rugby
Warwickshire CV21 2PJ

Postnatal support

The Active Birth Centre
Runs a variety of postnatal yoga and exercise classes. Call for information about teachers and classes.
Tel: 0171 561 9006

Association for Postnatal Illness
Send an SAE for information and useful leaflets about postnatal depression.
25 Jerdan Place
London SW6 1BE
Tel: 0171 386 0868

Exploring Parenthood
Offers a parents' advice line, group counselling and discussion with the aim of helping to alleviate stress and supporting families. Open to all parents, natural or adoptive.
4 Ivory Place
20a Treadgold Street
London W11 4BP
Tel: 0171 221 4471

Meet-A-Mum Association (MAMA)
Can put you in touch with other mothers and groups in your local area for socialising and support to help alleviate isolation, loneliness or depression.
26 Avenue Road
London SE25 4DX
Tel: 0181 771 5595

National Childbirth Trust (NCT)
As well as offering a wide variety of social opportunities to meet other new parents in your local area, the NCT runs postnatal exercise classes and discussion groups where you can talk over your concerns. You don't have to be an NCT member to join in the social activities, only if you want to take a more active role in the organisation.

In addition, trained breastfeeding counsellors can provide you with helpful information and support backed up by the latest research if your baby's crying seems to be linked to his feeding.

The NCT's national special experiences register can put you in touch with parents all over the country who have had a baby who cries excessively. It can also put you in touch with parents whose babies have eczema, learning disabilities, physical disabilities or other special needs. Telephone 0181 992 8637 and ask to be put in touch with the person who currently holds the register.

Many local NCT groups have meetings for parents whose babies have been born by caesarean section. As having a caesarean can bring particular problems in the early days when you are adjusting to your new baby, you may find these groups of value as they will enable you to meet other mothers who know what you are going through. In addition, many branches run support groups for women who have, or have had, postnatal depression. Some will also be able to put you in touch with other local parents who have had postnatal depression who can talk to you on a mother-to-mother basis.

If you don't know the number of your local branch, first try looking in the telephone book under NCT. The membership secretary will be able to tell you what's on offer in your area. If you can't find a listing, call NCT headquarters on 0181 992 8637 and they will be able to put you in touch.

Alexandra House
Oldham Terrace
London W3 6NH
Tel: 0181 992 8637

ParentAbility

Offers support and local contacts for parents with disabilities.
Alexandra House
Oldham Terrace
London W3 6NH
Tel: 0181 992 8637

Parent Network

Runs nationwide courses on parenting skills and Parent Link support groups.
2 Winchester House
Kennington Park
11 Cranmer Road
London SW9 6EJ
Tel: 0171 735 1214
Fax: 0171 735 4692

Premature babies

BLISS

(Baby Life Support Systems)
Provides neonatal equipment, specialist nurse training and support for parents of special care babies.
17–21 Emerald Street
London WC1N 3QL
Tel: 0171 831 9393
Helpline: 0500 618140 Mon–Fri 10.30am–4.30pm

Single parents

While the other organisations and resources listed here can be valuable to all parents, there are also some that single parents may find of particular benefit.

Home–Start UK
Trained advisers can visit you in your home and offer support in times of stress.
2 Salisbury Road
Leicester LE1 7QR
Tel: 0116 233 9955

Gingerbread
Gingerbread offers support and advice for single parents.
Tel: 0171 336 8183 for details of your nearest support group
Tel: 0171 336 8184 for their advice line

Twins (and more)

Twins and Multiple Births Association (TAMBA)
PO Box 30
Little Sutton
South Wirral L66 1TH
Tel: 0870 121 4000
Fax: 0870 121 4001
TAMBA supports families with twins, triplets or more,

individually, through local Twins Clubs and specialist support groups, and promotes public and professional awareness of their needs. Leaflets, booklets, books and magazine available. Access to professional information through the Health & Education Group. Specialist support for families with triplets or more; special needs; one-parent families; families who have lost one or more of a multiple birth set; adoptive parents; parents expecting or who have twins or more as a result of fertility treatment; and adult twins. Individual professional support available from a team of honorary consultants. Confidential telephone listening, information and support service (TAMBA Twinline: see opposite).

Further reading

This is not an exhaustive list of all the books that can help you explore further on a particular aspect. You will be able to find many more in your local library, and those books, in turn, will recommend further books. There are many different attitudes to parents, parenting, babies and crying, and it is only by getting a 'flavour' of each author that you can decide whether what they say makes sense for you and your family. In many cases, we give the date of the original edition here so that you can see when the book was first written. There may have been reprints and new editions since.

We also include references to some of the findings about crying mentioned in the text.

Chapter 1   Why do babies cry?

Sheila Kitzinger (1989) *The Crying Baby*, Penguin
A full discussion of the causes of crying and the results it can have for a family, looked at not only in the context of the individuals concerned, but also in the wider context of the social and political considerations within our culture.

Jane Moody, Jane Britten and Karen Hogg (1996) *Breastfeeding Your Baby*, NCT Publishing
A full discussion of the physiology and practicalities of breastfeeding, with much useful information about its benefits and fact files to help you understand why things might not be so smooth in the early days. There are also useful sections on feeding twins and premature babies.

Chapter 2   Finding the right approach

Penney Hames (1998) *Sleep*, NCT Publishing
A detailed manual covering all aspects of sleep and strategies for dealing with sleep problems.

Jo Douglas and Naomi Richman (1989) *My Child Won't Sleep!*, Penguin
A short manual with valuable strategies for coping and curing.

Richard Ferber (1985) *Solve Your Child's Sleep Problems*, Dorling Kindersley
A book that examines all aspects of children and sleep, with detailed guidance and reassurance for those who are thinking of using the 'controlled crying' method.

Christopher Green (1989) *Babies! A Parent's Guide to Surviving (and Enjoying) Baby's First Year*, Simon & Schuster
A practical guide to coping with baby basics, including crying, written in a forthright manner to which some parents will warm, others will not.

Angela Henderson (1997) *The Good Sleep Guide* (available by post from ABC Health Guides, 12 Moor Green, Neston, Corsham, Wiltshire SN13 9SG. Tel: 01225 812048 to check current price)
This is a brief, practical handbook which takes parents at their wits' end step by step through solving a variety of sleep problems.

Deborah Jackson (1989) *Three in a Bed*, Bloomsbury
Advocates the benefits and advantages to the whole family of co-sleeping. It may give you food for thought if you have doubts about bed-sharing with your baby.

Heather Lister (1993) 'A good feed', *New Generation*, March issue (available from NCT Library, at main NCT address.)
Looks in more depth at the idea of spacing out feeds in the early days as a way of avoiding 'colic' and crying.

The NSPCC produces a useful free leaflet called *Handle with care*. It contains helpful guidance on safe ways of holding and caring for your baby. Send an SAE to: NSPCC Publications, 42 Curtain Road, London EC2A 3NH.

Chapter 3   Looking after yourself

Sarah Clement (1991) *The Caesarean Experience*, Pandora (2nd edn 1995)
A full account of the physical and emotional repercussions of having a caesarean section which may help parents to understand their own needs and recovery, and the impact that the procedure can have on a baby.

Christopher Clulow (ed.) (1996) *Partners Becoming Parents*, Sheldon Press
Contains a useful essay on why so many couples begin to argue after the arrival of a baby which may help you put your own relationship in perspective.

Katarina Dalton (1989) *Depression After Childbirth*, Oxford University Press
An overview of the illness, with information about how progesterone treatment may help prevent its recurrence.

Sheila Kitzinger (1994) *The Year After Childbirth*, Oxford University Press
The first year in all its practical, emotional and social effects on the baby, the parents and the wider family.

Katherine Holdsworth (1997) 'The crying game', *New Generation*, March issue
A report on the study into infant crying carried out by a team headed by Ian St James-Roberts at the Thomas Coram Research Unit, University of London, written by one of the mothers who took part in the study. This study showed, among other things, that babies whose mothers held them most in the early weeks cried far less at 15 months than babies whose mothers held them least.

Mike Lilley (1996) *Successful Single Parenting*, How To Books
This covers all angles of being a single parent, including information on dealing with stress and widening your social life.

Fiona Marshall (1993) *Coping with Postnatal Depression*, Sheldon Press
A full account of the whole spectrum of postnatal illness with practical strategies for managing and recovering; useful not only for sufferers but also for their partners and supporters.

Rozsika Parker (1995) *Torn in Two: The Experience of Maternal Ambivalence*, Virago
A psychoanalytic exploration of how mothers can both 'love' and 'hate' their children simultaneously.

Anna McGrail (1998) *You and Your New Baby*, NCT Publishing
A handbook for the first few months of being a family, covering adjusting to life with a new baby, your body after the birth, postnatal depression, and your needs as a couple.

Heather Welford (1998) *Postnatal Depression*, NCT Publishing
An in-depth, practical approach to postnatal depression.

A free leaflet, *Help is at hand*, is available from the Royal College of Psychiatrists, produced as part of its Defeat Depression campaign. It gives straightforward, concise information on the range of symptoms and different types of treatment, and explains the avenues through which you can seek help and how you can help yourself. For a copy, send an SAE to:
Help is at Hand
17 Belgrave Square
London SW1X 8PG

Chapter 4   Survival strategies

Miranda Castro (1992) *Homoeopathy for Mother and Baby*, Macmillan
A comprehensive guide to the subject and guidance for using remedies at home.

Penelope Leach (1977) *Baby and Child*, Penguin (new edn 1996)
Along with masses of practical baby-care advice, this book also contains useful sections that chart the developing skills of a baby and lots of suggestions on 'games' you can play together at the various stages, starting from birth.

Gabriel Pinto and Murray Feldman (1996) *Homoeopathy for Children*, Thorsons
Gives the background and philosophy behind the subject as well as a variety of case histories which show how various remedies might be chosen and might help.

Peter Walker (1995) *Baby Massage*, Piatkus
A detailed, well-illustrated companion that will take you through the techniques.

Videos

Katie May's Video Guide to Baby Massage
Available from KTMC Productions, Woodbine Cottage, Pye Corner, Hambrook, Bristol BS16 1SE. Tel: 01454 776831 for details of price and postage.

Peter Walker, *DIY Step-by-Step Guide to Baby Massage*
Available to order through stores and also through NCT Maternity Sales Ltd, Burnfield Avenue, Glasgow G46 7TL. Tel: 0141 633 5552

Chapter 5   Special situations

T. Markestad (1997) 'Use of sucrose as a treatment for infant colic', *Archives of Diseases in Childhood*, 76 (4): 356–7

Blisslink/Nippers (1995) *Going Home: Taking your Special Care Baby Home*
A booklet for parents of premature babies available free of charge by sending an SAE to: BLISS, 17–21 Emerald Street, London WC1N 3QL.

Elizabeth Bryan (1996) *Twins, Triplets and More*, Multiple Births Foundation
Every aspect of multiple births explored in a friendly and readable style with valuable practical information.

Chapter 6   As your baby grows . . .

Robin Skinner and John Cleese (1988) *Families and How to Survive Them*, Fontana
A very readable book on how the arrival of a baby means psychological adjustments for all concerned (including the baby) which can help shed light on the emotional strains and stresses of the early months . . . and years.

Libby Purves (1987) *How Not to be a Perfect Mother*, Fontana
A fresh and entertaining perspective on parenting from the front line, which may be just the thing to cheer you up when the crying is getting you down.

Index

accepting 110–12
Active Birth Centre 148
acupuncture 145
  and teething 21–2
alcohol 75
almond oil 83
anger
  coping with feelings of
    63–6
  directed towards the
    partner 52–4
'angry' babies 12
anxious mothers 10
aromatherapy 85, 90–2,
  146
Association of
    Breastfeeding
    Mothers 142
Association for Postnatal
    Illness 149

'baby blues' 39–41
baby bouncers 72
back-carriers 70
bathtime 82
bed-sharing 30, 37, 73–4

birth trauma 8–9, 17–18
  and cranial osteopathy
    93, 94
BLISS (Baby Life Support
    Systems) 151
boredom 100–1
bottle-feeding 10, 19,
    23–5
  and dairy-free diets 97,
    99
  first- and second-stage
    milk 25
  twins or more 125
  water for making up
    bottles 99
  and wind 27
breastfeeding 19–24, 25
  at night 33, 35
  and babies' need for
    food 5–6
  and bed-sharing 73
  colostrum 5
  and comfort sucking
    21–2, 81
  and crying 10
  and diet 97, 98, 99

discomforts associated
    with 2
  foremilk and hindmilk
    20–1
  and the need to suck 8
  premature babies 129
  support groups 142–3
  twins or more 125
  and wind 27
Breastfeeding Network
    143
breathing difficulties 14,
    15
British Acupuncture
    Council 145
British Association for
    Counselling 148
British Chiropractic
    Association 146
British Homoeopathic
    Association 146
British Register of
    Complementary
    Practitioners 145
burning essential oils
    91–2

caesarean section babies 150, 158

car journeys 76–7

carriers 69–72

character of the baby 11–13

checklist 4

childbirth
  birth trauma 8–9, 17–18, 93, 94
  recovering from 1–2

chiropractic 95, 146

clingy babies 28–9, 61, 73

colic 49–50, 52, 90, 113–19
  barrier 16, 118–19
  and chiropractic 95
  and cranial osteopathy 93
  and dairy-free diets 96–7
  and feeding 115
  sugar solution 117–18, 162

communication skills of babies 3

Complementary Medical Association 145

complementary therapies 144–5

controlled crying 33–6, 38, 123

cot death risk 32

counselling 148
  NCT breastfeeding counsellors 24, 142, 150

cranial osteopathy 93–5

craniosacral therapy 95

CRY-SIS helpline 104–5, 143

crying it out 81

dairy-free diets 95–9, 138

dental decay 80

depression ('baby blues') 39–40
  see also postnatal depression

diets
  dairy-free 95–9, 138
  iron-rich 43–5

difficult births see birth trauma

disabled babies 131–2, 150

doctors
  reasons for calling the doctor 14–16
  see also GPs (general practitioners)

Down's syndrome babies 132

driving 76–7

dummies 33, 77, 78–81
  and colic 117

eczema 123, 150

exercise
  for new mothers 50–1
  postnatal classes 110, 148

exhaustion, long-term 57–60

Exploring Parenthood 149

family therapy 137

fathers
  anxiety and stress 2, 40
  see also partners

feeding 19–25
  at night 29, 30, 33, 35, 38
  babies' need for food 5–6
  and colic 115
  further reading on 157
  giving solids 10, 100
  new-born babies 5, 19–20
  premature babies 129

'schedule' feeding 19
  twins or more 125
  and weight gain 23
  and wind 27
  see also bottle-feeding; breastfeeding

feelings towards the baby 60–6, 159

'feet to foot' position 7, 32

finger sucking 77–8

first babies 10

food allergies 99

getting out of the house 102–3
  with twins 127–8

Gingerbread 152

GPs (general practitioners)
  advice and support from 16, 35
  calling the doctor 14–16
  and homoeopathy 89
  and sedatives 76
  and support services 103–4, 141

gripe waters 27, 75

'growing out of' crying 134

guilt, coping with feelings of 58–60, 66, 106

health visitors
  advice and support from 16, 65
  clinics 110
  and controlled crying 36
  and dairy-free diets 97, 98
  and disabled babies 132
  and feeding advice 22, 23, 24, 25
  and sedatives 76
  and single parents 57

and support services
103–4, 141
and twins or more 126
helplines 65, 104–5,
143–4
herbal remedies 90, 146
'high-need' babies 12–13
and colic 115
holding the baby 28–9,
158
Holistic Association of
Reflexologists 148
Home-Start UK 152
homoeopathy 88–9,
146–7
further reading on 160,
161
hospitals, homoeopathic
89
'hostile' mothers 10

Infacol Colic Helpline
144
International Federation
of Aromatherapists
146
iron-rich diet 43–5

La Leche League 143
late onset crying 16
lavender oil 91
leaving the baby to cry
30–1, 81
libraries 102
life-changing events 1–2
lone parents see single
parents
lullabies 86, 130

machinery noise 86–7
massage 82–4, 92, 147,
161
videos on 84, 161
Meet-A-Mum Association
(MAMA) 149
'miserable' babies 11

mother-and-baby groups
108, 109
mothers
and birth trauma 8–9,
17–18
and breastfeeding 19–24
dairy-free diets 95–9,
138
depression 39–41
exercise 50–1
feelings towards the
baby 61–6
iron-rich diets 43–5
and long-term
exhaustion 57–60
re-establishing the
couple relationship
52–7
recovering from the
birth 1–2
sharing the load 45–52
socialising 106–10
and tiredness 41–3
music 85–6
myths about crying babies
9–11

National Institute of
Medical Herbalists
146
NCT (National
Childbirth Trust)
149–50
breastfeeding counsellors
24, 142, 150
national special
experiences register
105, 150
postnatal exercise classes
110
social events 105, 106
needs of babies 4–9
adapting responses to
133
checklist of 127
nervous babies 12

neurological shift (babies
at six weeks) 3
new-born babies
amount of crying 4
carriers for 70
feeding 5, 19–20
sleeping 29
swaddling 69, 130
night-time
bathtime routine 82
distinguishing between
night and day 29–30
driving 76–7
feeding 29, 30, 33, 35,
38
settling the baby 32–3
temperature of baby's
bedroom 6
transitions 37–8, 79–80
see also sleeping
nightmares 136
noise 86–8

Osteopathic Centre for
Children 147
osteopathy 147–8
outdoor activities 102–3

Parent Network 151
ParentAbility 151
Parentline 144
partners
and bed-sharing with
the baby 73, 74
relationships with 52–7
further reading on
158
sharing feelings with
65–6
sharing the load with
36, 46, 49–50
postnatal depression 40–1,
54
'baby blues' 39–40
further reading on 158,
159, 160

NCT support groups
for 150
puerperal psychosis 40
postnatal support 148–51
pregnancy, stress during
10
premature babies 128–31,
151, 162

reflexology 95–6, 148
reflux 16, 115
relatives
help from 47–8, 55
and twins or more
124–5, 126
rocking the baby 32, 72–3

second or third babies
137–9
sedatives 75–6
self-blame 139–40
Serene helpline 143–4
settling the baby 32–6
sexual relations 55
sharing the load 29, 45–52
with relatives 47–8, 55
and twins or more
124–5, 126
with your partner 36,
46, 49–50
see also support services
singing to the baby 84, 86
single parents 45, 57
further reading for 159
support organisations
for 152

sleep training 33–6
sleeping 29–31
babies' need to sleep 8
bed-sharing 30, 37,
73–4, 157
further reading on
156–7
safe sleeping 7, 32
settling the baby 32–6
and twins 126–7
see also night-time
slings 28, 70, 71–2
smiling babies 3
socialising 106–10
with twins 127–8
Society of Homoeopaths
147
solid food 10, 100
'spoiling' the baby, fears
about 13–14
stimulation
babies' need for 7
visual 100–3
sucking, babies' need to
suck 8, 77–81
sugar solution for colic
117–18, 162
support services 141–4
from GPs and health
visitors 103–4, 141
swaddling 69, 130
swimming pools 51, 102

talking it through 136–7
TAMBA Twinline 144,
153

teething 120–2
and dummies 79
telephone helplines 65,
104–5, 143–4
temperature of baby's
bedroom 6
thirst 25
thumb-sucking 80, 136
tiredness 41–3
and bed-sharing 73–4
long-term exhaustion
57–60
triplets 125, 152–3
twins (and more) 124–8
feeding 125
further reading on
162
support from relatives
124–5, 126
TAMBA (Twins and
Multiple Births
Association) 152–3
Twinline 144, 153
Twins Clubs 126

unexplained crying 9–11

vacuum cleaner noise 86–7
videos, on baby massage
161
visual stimulation 100–3

water, for making up
bottles 99
wind 26–7, 115
'womb music' tapes 87